Under Minnesota Skies

John and Dorothy Hondl Family History and Farm Memories

As told by their daughters
Bernadette Hondl Thomasy and Colleen Hondl Gengler
Assisted by Nadine Hondl

Bernadette Hondl Thomasy

Colleen Hondl Gengler

June 2015
This book is a work of nonfiction

Photographs by/or in the collections of the Authors unless otherwise noted.
Sarah Selz, Editor
Cover design and layout by Lawrence Fox

I Street Press, Sacramento Public Library
828 I Street, Sacramento, CA 95814
(916) 264-2777
istreet@saclibrary.org

Library of Congress Control Number: 2015948577

ISBN: 978-1519101600

street
press
A COMMUNITY WRITING
& PUBLISHING CENTER

Under Minnesota Skies

John and Dorothy Hondl
Family History and
Farm Memories

Foreword

Research for this family history actually began more than thirty-five years ago. In the 1980s, during visits to her childhood farm home in Minnesota, Bernadette Hondl Thomasy began recording family stories. Her father John Hondl would reminisce about the early years of farming and how he and his "old man" did things. Trained as a journalist, Bernadette felt there was a story there and started taking notes and asking questions of both John and her mother Dorothy Spindler Hondl. Gradually, Bernadette put these memories and some of her own recollections into a document that grew and grew. Her mother and sisters, Nadine Hondl and Colleen Hondl Gengler, read and enjoyed these efforts.

In 2002, John's death from cancer left a big hole in the family. During a visit to the Hondl farm to help the family plan a memorial service, a priest thoughtfully remarked that he saw "John's footprints everywhere"– in the dozens of arbor vitae and evergreen trees planted, the modern buildings strategically placed in the yard, field roads worn to powder by countless tractor trips, fences built and rebuilt. John had lived his entire eighty-nine years at this place, with sixty years as owner and operator, cultivating and shaping the land season after season. But, he would no longer be a source for stories about the farm he loved.

His wife and daughters who had walked and worked alongside John hoped to find a way to keep his legacy of the land alive for future generations. They felt this story was significant because the farm had been in the Hondl family for more than a century. In 2010, as Dorothy turned ninety years of age, the Hondl daughters realized they needed to tap their mother's memories further while she was still able to share them. Youngest daughter Colleen, who for some time had been contemplating researching the family's ancestry, got involved.

After she retired in 2012, Colleen reinvigorated the Hondl story project by writing about her own experiences growing up on the farm. She enlisted help from her sister Nadine who contributed portions as well, with Dorothy verifying details as she recalled them. Colleen dug further

i

into the genealogy of John's and Dorothy's families. She discovered some surprising results, helping the Hondl women more fully understand their history and their connections to the Czech roots and culture of their neighbors, friends and classmates in Steele County, Minnesota.

The high point of their discoveries came during a trip to Eastern Europe in the summer of 2014 when Colleen and her husband Don spent several days in the Czech Republic. They traveled about 100 miles east of Prague to the small villages of Dlouhá Trebová, Rudoltice and Ribníck in the Pardubice region. As Colleen walked in these villages from which great-grandparents on both sides of the family came, it was easy to see how her ancestors could have adapted to their new home in America. The region, with its gently rolling green hills, pockets of trees, small rivers and beautiful blue skies dotted with clouds, clearly felt like Minnesota.

The family history that follows is a summation of these efforts. The goal was to learn about the past while recording some of the people and events that shaped the lives of John and Dorothy and their three daughters. Part One describes the ancestors of John and Dorothy, as well as the couple's growing up years, marriage and building a life together with their three daughters on the Hondl land. In Part Two the daughters tell their personal stories about growing up in a close-knit Midwestern farm family in the 1950s and 1960s and how it prepared them for adult lives. Gathered together these experiences connect this family in a special way, a harvest of memories preserved for future generations.

Contents

John and Dorothy Hondl Family Tree

Jan Hondl
1838-1907

Anna Groh
1836-1905

John Haubenschild
1853-1910

Frances Groh
1852-1933

Frank W. Spindler
1849-1902

Anna Miller
1853-1902

Ignac Kubista
1830-1914

Rosalie Basharna (Pisorna)
1844-1915

Anton J. Hondl
1870-1949

Karolina(Lena) Haubenschild
1881-1951

Frank J. Spindler
1875-1960

Agnes J. Kubista
1880-1938

John Hondl
1912-2002

Dorothy S. Spindler
1920-

Nadine Hondl
1943-

Bernadette Hondl Thomasy
1944-

Colleen Hondl Gengler
1951-

Introduction

This family history focuses on John Frank Hondl and Dorothy Spindler Hondl. It spans multiple generations, beginning with the stories of John's and Dorothy's ancestors who first came to the United States from Europe in the late 1860s (Dorothy's maternal grandparents) and in the 1880s, even before it became commonplace to enter the United States through Ellis Island, the great welcoming gateway for so many newcomers to America. It then moves down through the generations and ultimately ends with perspectives from John and Dorothy's daughters, Nadine Hondl, Bernadette Hondl Thomasy and Colleen Hondl Gengler. All of these generations play a key role in this family history. However, this is not just a history of people; it is also a history of place. As such, it is also the story of the Hondl farm, documenting how the farm took shape across the generations and how it became central to life for the Hondls.

The story of the farm, around which much of this family history revolves, begins with Jan (John) Hondl. Recently emigrated from Bohemia, Jan purchased a piece of land (South ½ of the Northwest Quarter of Section 19, Township 106, Range 19 West) on May 21, 1881 in Steele County, Minnesota. Jan, as well as Dorothy's and John's other ancestors, were most likely farmers in the small communities and villages from which they came, and they brought this farming legacy with them when they came to Minnesota. With this purchase, Jan planted his roots in America for the present-day Hondls, including his great granddaughters Nadine, Bernadette and Colleen. Although Jan of course never knew these three women, he may have had future generations in mind when he left Bohemia, which had been the scene of centuries of war and contention between neighboring military and political powers, to find a better life. Today's generation is certainly influenced by those decisions made more than 150 years ago to establish a new life in America and eventually in Steele County, Minnesota.

In 1896 and the following years, the farm expanded from its original parcel. Jan's son Anton purchased additional adjacent land, forming the current 394-acre Hondl farm in Aurora Township. Then, in 1941, Anton's son John Hondl and his wife Dorothy began renting shares of the land from his father, thus continuing the family tradition of farming. After Anton died in 1949, John and Dorothy continued to operate the farm on shares until John's mother Lena passed away in 1951. Following Lena's estate auction, John and Dorothy purchased the Hondl farm.

Hondl farm site in Steele County, Minnesota, 1949.

Even though they had already been renting the land from his parents, buying the farm was a huge financial decision for John and Dorothy, especially since John was the third youngest in a family of eight. Traditionally, the oldest son had first chance at taking over the family farm; however, in the Hondl family, John's oldest brother was already established. The purchase would prove integral to the lives of John, Dorothy, and their three daughters, starting what would become a sixty-year effort by the Hondl family to improve and cultivate the land. Over the years, tiling improved drainage for better crop yields and some grassland was plowed for more tillable acres. Crop rotation of soybeans and corn plus a periodic cover crop of alfalfa returned nutrients to the soil. In addition, new crop storage facilities and buildings to house livestock and machinery were constructed. Through these efforts, John and Dorothy created challenging yet deeply satisfying lives for their family These efforts, intertwined with the experiences of each family member, are the central story of this family history.

Although this family history does revolve in large part around the Hondl farm, farming is certainly not the only important personal or historical theme. There is a need to know where one comes from both literally and figuratively as a way to better know one's self, and this need extends beyond understanding any one place or time. As such, the history ends with looking forward, detailing how the daughters left the farm to start independent lives of their own as John and Dorothy grew older, but also backwards, towards revisiting the places from which their ancestors came. Through pointing in multiple directions at once, this family history aims to explore how history and traditions, both forgotten and upheld, come together to shape the past and the present.

Part One: Side by Side -
John and Dorothy

John and Dorothy Hondl, wedding portrait, November 26, 1941.

1

Valuing the Land -
John Frank Hondl's Story

The Haubenschilds - John's Maternal Family

John Hondl's maternal grandparents both came from what was then known as Bohemia, a part of the Austro-Hungarian Empire, now the Czech Republic. John Haubenschild, John's maternal grandfather, was born November 25, 1853, in Ribnick. Franzes (Frances) Groh, John's maternal grandmother, was born on November 25, 1852, also in Ribnick, as the second of five children. John and Frances were married in 1871 in nearby Rudoltice. Although born in Bohemia, John Haubenschild and Frances Groh were of German heritage. Over the centuries, Germans had moved into many areas of Bohemia; it was common for entire villages to be German-speaking.

Shortly after their marriage, John and Frances moved to Ukraine which, at the time, was ruled by Russia. The Czar was giving away free land and the Haubenschilds hoped to take advantage of the opportunity. They journeyed from Ribnick to Alexandra on the Krym, also known as the Crimean Peninsula, which was located near the Black Sea and was a part of Ukraine. The journey was over 1,000 miles and would have been very difficult to undertake at the time. While in Ukraine, John was in the Russian army during a time of peace. Perhaps the army's need for soldiers was so critical it allowed the soldiers' spouses to move with them. John and Frances may have been able to combine farming with his military duties while in Ukraine.

John appears to have been a multi-talented man. In addition to military duty and farming, the *Groh Family History* indicates that John was a craftsman in woodworking and hand carving.[1] No doubt those skills were useful throughout his life.

While living in Ukraine, John and Frances started their family with their first child born in 1872. Records indicate the first four children including Karolina (Lena, John Hondl's mother) were born at Alexandra on the Krym with a fifth child born at Odessa, Russia, in September 1885.

After fourteen years in the Ukraine, John, Frances and their children set sail for the United States on the ship SSEMMS. They landed in New York City on November 25, 1885. It must have been daunting for the Haubenschilds to endure the long trip with five children from age 13 to a baby just over two months old; yet, this is what many immigrant families did. After first settling in Wisconsin, John and Frances relocated to Steele County, Minnesota, on sixty acres of land in Aurora Township. In 1897, they purchased 920 acres in Summit Township, known as the Kelley Farm. The property was located near Ellendale, Minnesota and was bought for $19,000 plus an additional $5,000 for eighty cows and equipment. They paid $100 a month to the seller, Thomas Kelley. Besides working as farmers, John and his sons owned a complete set of ditching equipment, which they used throughout Summit Township. John also owned stock in the Farmers' Elevator and the Farmers' Creamery at Ellendale according to the *History of Rice and Steele Counties, Minnesota.*[2]

While in Minnesota, John and Frances had five more children. This brought them to a total of ten children: four sons and six daughters. In addition, it is believed that they had an infant son who died at birth and is buried at the north end of Holy Trinity Catholic Church Cemetery marked by an iron cross. The cemetery is at Litomysl, a small community in Somerset Township, Steele County. There is no other record of the infant son.

Over time, John Haubenschild, who stood five feet six inches tall, came to be considered a prominent member of the community. He became a United States citizen on June 14, 1897 and exercised his political preferences as a Democrat. According to his obituary John was held in high esteem by his fellow citizens and always met his obligations.[3] John also maintained his Catholic heritage from his start in the small Bohemian villages, even though the Orthodox Church may have been prominent there, throughout his time in Minnesota. John died on December 24, 1910, in Ellendale. His gravesite is located at the Holy Trinity Catholic Church Cemetery with the name "Howbenschild" on the gravestone. It is unknown just how that spelling came to be inscribed on the headstone. His wife Frances died twenty-three years later on September 23, 1933, also in Ellendale.

John and Frances Haubenschild family, John Hondl's maternal grandparents. 1902: John's mother, Lena, back row, far right; Uncle Paul, center, in sailor suit.

Karolina, John's Mother

The second Haubenschild daughter was Karolina (Lena), John Hondl's mother and paternal grandmother to Nadine, Bernadette and Colleen. She was born May 19, 1881 in the Krym, part of the Russian Ukraine. When she was four years old, in 1885, she emigrated to the United States with her family. One can only speculate what the trip must have been like for Karolina at such a young age. Perhaps she was given the task of amusing her two-year-old brother while her mother Frances took care of the young Haubenschild baby during the long voyage.

Paul, an Inspiring Uncle

One of Lena's brothers, Leopold (Paul) Haubenschild, was a favorite uncle of John's. Paul was born March 2, 1894, in Ellendale, Minnesota. He served in France during WWI and moved to Circle, Montana, in 1920. The background of Uncle Paul's move to the West makes for an interesting family story. The story was captured in the history of the Groh family:

> During prohibition days, two boys, Paul and Tony [Paul's brother], left Minnesota after the "Feds" moved in on their "Rum

Running Still" which was behind a cemetery on rolling ground hidden from view, near their Minnesota farm. They had a back way out and as the Feds moved in they left by the back way to escape. They didn't return to Minnesota because they were "wanted". Tony ended up in Canada and Uncle Paul first came to Odessa, Washington, and stayed for a while with his sister, Mary, then returned as far as Circle, Montana.[4]

In Circle, Paul became a wheat farmer and cattle rancher owning six sections or 3,840 acres. This occupation lasted for the rest of his life. In 1938, after eighteen years in Montana, Paul married Mathilda Job, a registered nurse, in Jordan, Montana. Mathilda died shortly after their son, Paul, Jr., was born. She is buried in Circle.

John and Dorothy made several trips to Montana to visit Uncle Paul and his son. John may have developed his love for wheat farming and raising cattle through these visits. John was also inspired and intrigued by the American West and Native American lore and culture, which Uncle Paul passed on with enthusiasm gained through firsthand experiences.

One incident in particular shows how significant Uncle Paul was to John. In a diary Bernadette kept during her teenage years, she noted that on June 19, 1960, her father John was excited to learn his Uncle Paul was in the Owatonna area to spend time with relatives. John and Dorothy drove to various homes trying to locate Paul but were not successful. Three days later, the whole family was thrilled when Uncle Paul arrived at the Hondl farm for an hour and a half visit. The Hondls did not receive a lot of visitors and to have someone from Montana at the farm was remarkable. Bernadette recalled that her father did not have many heroes (Franklin Delano Roosevelt and John Wayne were two), but Uncle Paul was definitely someone John greatly admired.

Uncle Paul died on March 20, 1968, in Circle. Paul Jr. eventually moved back to Blooming Prairie, Minnesota.

The Hondls – John's Paternal Family

Anton J. Hondl, John's father, was born October 29, 1870, in Bohemia. His family may also have been from Ribnick. In 1880 he came to the United States with his father Jan Hondl (1838-1907) and his mother Anna Groh Hondl (1836-1905). According to the 1900 United States Census, both of Anton's parents were also born in Bohemia, where they were married in 1858.[5] They had seven children, one of whom passed away sometime prior to 1900. After arriving in the United States, Jan, Anna and their children first settled in Columbus, Wisconsin for one winter before moving to Minnesota. In 1881, they purchased 200 acres in Section 19, Aurora Township in Steele County, later adding sixty more acres.

In 1890, Anton left Minnesota to spend three years working in California along with a friend named John Plotz. John Hondl had vivid memories of the stories his father told about those adventurous years. John had always wanted to see the Stockton area where his father had toiled on a large wheat farm. Anton talked about having a Chinese cook, which certainly would have been a novel experience for him. He also told of working with forty-two horses and mules in teams that pulled huge combines. Anton recalled eating peach pie almost every day and said he saw women only about three times in three years. Two of the three occasions took place when he was asked to drive into town to bring the dressmaker to the farmer's home. She would stay for a week and sew clothing for the family.

Anton was paid in gold and accumulated $1,000 in three years – a large sum of money in those days. However, things were not going quite as well back in Minnesota. His father wrote to him, asking him to return home because they were in danger of losing the family farm in Steele County. Anton came back to Minnesota and continued to work on the farm, which he eventually took over. John recalled his father summing up his California experience by saying, "California was fine for women and children, but hell on men and mules."

In spite of those dire words, John sometimes said he wished his father had stayed in California — then he would have grown up there. To live in California was the goal of many Midwesterners (and still is today). In the 1930s and 1940s the pioneering spirit remained strong among young men, particularly following the grim reality of the Great Depression and the Dust Bowl. In later decades the desire to live "the California dream" with better weather, more fertile land and greater opportunities would continue to pull people from the Midwest and elsewhere in the United States. The vast western landscape and the lure of the ocean's unlimited horizons appealed to the human spirit in ways unknown in the Midwest.

The Marriage: Hondl-Haubenschild

Despite the great allure of the West, Anton did return to Minnesota and eventually married Karolina (Lena) Haubenschild, on November 22, 1898, in Aurora Township. Lena was seventeen while Anton was twenty-eight, which would have been considered "old" for him to be getting married. A year later, according to United States Census records, Anton and Lena had no children and Anton was listed as owning a farm with a mortgage. The record also indicates that both Anton and Lena could read, write and speak English.[6]

Anton and Lena would go on to have a family of eight children. John Frank Hondl was born October 24, 1912, the third youngest in the family. His brothers and sisters included: Helen (Renchin), Benita (Ressler), Clarence, Myrtle (Ressler), Clement (who later lived with John, Dorothy and family), Loretta (Haberman) and George (who lived on the farm southeast of John's farm). According to a county history, Anton was independent in his voting, a member of the M.W.A. Lodge, and a stockholder in the Pratt Creamery.[7] In 1941 Lena and Anton retired from their Aurora Township farm and moved to Owatonna, Minnesota. Anton died in 1949 and Lena in 1951. She is buried beside Anton in Sacred Heart Cemetery, Owatonna.

Growing Up

John did not speak much about his growing up years in part because his childhood was cut short and he had to focus on chores and working in the fields from the age of ten. A "work first, even on Sundays" attitude prevailed. One can imagine a household where the three older boys were kept busy with feeding and caring for animals, driving horses, picking corn by hand, hauling hay and completing all the farm work that was done manually. In this way, John was actually preparing himself for his life's work as a farmer. He developed a soft spot for horses and enjoyed caring for them so they would give their best effort when working in the field.

The Hondl family lived through the Great Depression and John recalled some lean times. As a son of the Depression, John learned that food was not to be wasted or taken for granted. He recalled having rendered lard sandwiches in his school lunch pail and sometimes going to bed hungry. Fresh fruit was considered such a luxury that only the girls in his family were allowed to eat the bananas.

While the Hondls were known to serve huge, delicious meals for threshing crews, the family's daily meals were very basic. Perhaps this is why later on John always wanted plenty of food on the table for his own family and knew that homemade was still the best. He also took an interest when his own family was planning special meals. For example, should the meat for Christmas dinner be goose, ham or turkey?

When John was about six years old, an event occurred in his family that made a big impression on him. The Hondls had been living in a small two-story house, which would have been crowded for the family of eight children. Therefore, they built a large five-bedroom addition with a living room and dining room onto the existing house. Unfortunately, the children were not allowed in the "fancy part" of the house, at least not on a daily basis. As was customary for the times, the formal dining room and parlor were reserved for guests. Lena, no doubt, was trying to protect the nice woodwork and leaded glass doors on the china cupboard and curio cabinets from the antics of four lively boys.

John did not mention many fun times, but his family did own a pair of cross-country skis and a sled. With plenty of Minnesota snow available, the brothers and sisters possibly spent many an afternoon having snowball fights or pulling one another on skis or a sled behind a horse. The skis remained at the Hondl farm over the years. In her travels to the Czech Republic, Colleen saw the exact same kind of wooden skis with a very wide tip end.

In the midst of hardships and busy farming life, John had only limited educational opportunities. John did attend Steele County District 58 School, a half mile south of the Hondl farm, but he was only allowed to complete the fourth grade. After that, he was expected to help fulltime on the farm. Even though his attendance there was cut short, John received certificates signed by his teachers and the county superintendent commending him for regularity of attendance and punctuality. The family still has several of the certificates. The family also has many Valentine's

Day cards that were given to John including two from his teacher Miss King.

Despite limited formal education, John was able to read the newspaper and do basic math computations. He was largely self-taught in whatever skills he needed to succeed in farming and often read farm publications and machinery manuals. In at least one instance, John might have felt sad about not being able to continue his education. He told the story of driving cattle into Owatonna to be loaded on the train for market. The typical route was on South Grove Street going past Owatonna High School. It so happened that the students

Valentine card given to John Hondl by his teacher, 1920.

were just getting out for lunch as the cattle were driven by, adding to the challenge of keeping the cattle going in the right direction. It must have pained John to think he would never be one of those students.

Would it have made a difference in John's life if he had had more formal education? It is difficult to speculate. He had excellent problem-solving skills, as did many farmers who used ingenuity and what was at hand to figure out solutions. For instance, he would fix a horse harness with available leather pieces. With a larger project later on, John devised a way to build a new bridge over a deep creek bed making things safer for heavier and newer machinery. John's native intelligence also took him to a level of trying new things, including being an early adopter of the newest machinery and eventually making the switch from dairy to beef cattle as described later.

John was quite successful in spite of only receiving a limited education, but he wanted more for his daughters and continually emphasized to them the importance of getting a good education. He may have recognized that education was a key to a future for his daughters who would have different vocations and ambitions. John was eager to see his daughters advance through high school, vocational school and college. John enjoyed celebrating their graduations and loved conversations about what his daughters were learning. John could not have been more excited about their accomplishments and eagerly shared them with friends and neighbors.

2

Finding Joy in Family –
Dorothy Susan Spindler's Story

The Kubistas - Dorothy's Maternal Family

Agnes J. Kubista, Dorothy's mother, was born in Somerset Township on February 22, 1880. Dorothy's grandfather, Ignac Kubista, was born January 1, 1830, in Dlouhá Třebová a small village in eastern Bohemia. Ignac came to America in 1867 with his first wife (name unknown) and two children. A third child was born in the United States, but his first wife died young, apparently in childbirth. Ignac then married Rosa Basharna (Pisorna), Dorothy's grandmother. She was born in the same district of Bohemia, on April 17, 1844. The Kubistas joined a large group of Czech immigrants settling in Steele County, as Michael Wolesky documents so effectively in his book *We Lack for Nothing Now: The Czech Settlement of Steele County, Minnesota*. The following is an excerpt from the book that details some of the strife early American farmers faced as they tried to make lives tied to the land:

> Ignac Kubista and his family settled in Somerset Township, in the area later known as Saco. They homesteaded 500 acres of land, but neglected to register the land as required by the homesteading law. Their family history says this happened because they could not afford to subscribe to the newspaper in which the notice to register was published. [8] In addition they did not read English and no one had told them about the registration requirement. As a result, someone else registered for part of their land and they lost about 200 wooded acres.
>
> Like other early farmers in the area, Ignac took his wheat to Faribault by ox cart to have it ground into flour. One time on the way home his oxen smelled the rain-swollen creek and rushed forward to drink from the creek. Ignac was unable to keep them

in check and the jouncing about caused all the freshly ground flour to spill on the ground. This was the creek just south of Owatonna, the future location of the Monterey Ballroom. [9]

Ignac and Rosalie Kubista, Dorothy's maternal grandparents, circa 1880s.
Courtesy Steele County Historical Society.

Ignac retired from farming in about 1897 because of failing health. He died on April 8, 1914. According to his obituary, "Mr. Kubista was an honest, upright man. He was very highly esteemed all thru this community."[10] Rosalie died of heart disease the following year on June 24. In her obituary, she is described as "an old and respected resident of this county."[11] Both are buried at the St. Wenceslaus Cemetery (Hrbitov-Sv-Vaclava) southwest of Owatonna. The cemetery and area around it is better known as Saco.

Frank J. and Agnes Spindler family, 1925. Back row, from left: Agnes, Frank, Charles, William, Helen: center row: Roselyn, Mary, John. Seated in chair, Dorothy.

The Spindlers - Dorothy's Paternal Family

Dorothy's father, Frank Joseph Spindler, was born December 23, 1875, in Bohemia. He came to the United States at the age of six with his parents, Anna Miller and Franz (Frank) Spindler, both born in Bohemia. Frank's parents, Dorothy's paternal grandparents, also came to the United States at the same time. The family route to America was through Prussia and then Bremen, Germany, the departure point for many ships carrying immigrants. They arrived in Baltimore on the ship Leipzig on April 30,

1881. Other members of the Spindler family may have come in earlier years.

The Marriage: Spindler-Kubista

Dorothy's parents, Frank Joseph Spindler and Agnes Josephine Kubista, were married August 23, 1898, when Agnes was eighteen. Dorothy Susan Spindler, the youngest of nine children, was born to Frank and Agnes September 4, 1920, in Owatonna. The Spindlers lived about three miles east of Pratt on a 160-acre farm in Havana and Aurora townships. Dorothy's family included brothers Frank, Charles, William and John and sisters Helen Kubista, Agnes Sommers, Roselyn Schrom and Mary Warner.

Growing Up

The Spindlers were a devout Catholic family, attending Sacred Heart Church in Owatonna. According to Dorothy, Sacred Heart then looked pretty much as it does today with its red brick exterior, off-white cement trim, twin spires and ornate interior. Overall, the church is reminiscent of some churches in present day Czech Republic. In snowy winters, she recalled the family going to church in a sleigh. They would be covered up with two heavy robes. In good weather, the nine and a half mile ride would have been pleasant with only the sounds of the horses and their harnesses jingling as the sleigh runners moved smoothly over the snow.

Dorothy remembered taking lunch to her father when he was out working in the fields. He suffered from ulcers and did not eat meat. He preferred noodles, bread and buttermilk. Dorothy carried the lunch in a tin pail, which was probably recycled from purchasing food at a store. Grandpa Spindler celebrated his Bohemian heritage by reading the Bohemian papers to keep up with the community back in Europe and with others who had immigrated to the United States. Dorothy said that her father was an excellent winemaker and often brewed a variety of wines including dandelion, mountain ash and rhubarb vintages. He would serve them on Sundays as a special treat for family and guests.

Dorothy also remembered helping her family with the fall corn harvest. First, they had to hand cut the cornstalks and then put them into shocks to dry. She and her brother would walk around the field to all the shocks, tying a rope around the top of each one. Both of them would pull hard to tighten the rope keeping the shock together.

The Spindler family spent a great deal of time baking, cooking and sewing for the large family as well as gardening and preserving foods for the winter. The women got together to make quilts and strip feathers for pillows, a task Dorothy said she did not care for. She did, however, appreciate the lively family gatherings with card playing and piano music. Her older brothers and sisters, who had started families of their own, invited their siblings to family picnics and holiday dinners. John's family, by contrast, did little socializing. Dorothy could not recall attending an extended family dinner with the Hondls, nor was there any card playing. John's siblings tended to go their own way once they left home.

One of Dorothy's childhood memories is the time she got scarlet fever. In December, she went to stay with her brother Charles and his wife Bertha to help care for their children. First Dorothy had a high fever. Eventually, she broke out with small itchy blisters, which actually helped her feel better. As a result of her illness, her brother's house was quarantined for three weeks; a sign was put on the door alerting visitors to stay away. Dorothy remembered Dr. Smersh coming to see her. He was a fixture in the lives of many Steele County families as a long time doctor in the area. Dorothy's brother Charles stayed separately from everyone else so that he could come and go. For Christmas that year, Dorothy recalled her parents rewarded her with her first wristwatch.

The Spindlers owned a piano and Dorothy could play a little by ear. Her sister Mary learned to play the piano by receiving instructions and sheet music through the mail. Dorothy, who practiced some of the same tunes, recalled that Mary had to send completed lessons back in the mail. Dorothy really enjoyed music and later wished she had inherited the family piano instead of the Spindler Singer treadle sewing machine. Her sister Mary got the piano. Dorothy did not like sewing very much and said she did not have the patience for it. Her own sewing was limited mostly to repairs of John's work overalls and shirts. However, she did show Nadine how to use the sewing machine and eventually all three daughters made good use of the machine despite its limited abilities. Manufactured in 1925 in Elizabeth, New Jersey, it could only sew in a straight line, no zig-zag option or buttonhole attachment.[12] Nadine and Colleen, especially, became expert seamstresses. Nadine took home economics in high school and sewed several dress and jacket ensembles. Colleen remembered going to Owatonna High School's Home Economics department to watch her big sister Nadine model her latest outfit in a class style show.

The Spindler family was fortunate to obtain electricity a few years earlier than their neighbors. Dorothy's brother John maintained a set of large, wet-cell batteries. John was quite proud of this responsibility as it allowed the family to do things like use an electric iron and heat water in the kitchen. There were limitations on how much equipment could be run off the battery system, but it still helped make household chores a little easier.

Dorothy excelled in grade school and wanted to become a teacher. At the District 26 School, she did well at spelling, reading and math. After graduating from the eighth grade, which is as far as the district schools went, both she and her sister Mary wanted to attend high school. Their father said "no" because none of the older brothers and sisters had done so. Likely there were many reasons that the Spindler siblings did not go to high school.

Dorothy Spindler, age eighteen, 1938.

Attendance in Owatonna would have meant boarding in town because it would not have been practical to make the daily trip from their home. There was no school bus at the time. Fewer "farm girls and boys" would have gone to high school at the time as compared to those living in town.

Meanwhile, Dorothy's mother Agnes developed throat cancer. Dorothy and Mary, as the youngest daughters still at home, had to perform more of the household duties that their mother could no longer accomplish. They also helped with outside chores as needed. Agnes died of throat cancer July 23, 1938, when Dorothy was just seventeen. A year later, her youngest brother John got married and set up housekeeping at the Spindler home place. It was tradition that a son would take over the family farm. With the new household established, both Dorothy and Mary had to find another place to live. It was a common situation at the time, one they had no choice but to accept. Their father, Frank, continued to live at the home farm.

Dorothy Works "In Town"

After she left home, Dorothy had several positions working for families "in town" as did several of her older sisters. It was commonplace for a family whose breadwinner was a businessman or professional to have hired help. In return for room and board and a small wage, the young woman would take care of the children, do household chores, cook and shop with the mistress of the house. Many young women from the farm got their first taste of urban life with these live-in jobs. Some of Dorothy's employers treated their workers more like servants and had the young women eat in the kitchen with the children. Other employers were more collaborative, like the woman who worked alongside Dorothy each spring to clean carpets, polish silverware and wax floors. Some of the names of families for whom Dorothy worked are still prominent in Owatonna.

Dorothy's first employer was the family of Vitus Hudrlik, who owned a furniture store and a funeral home. Dorothy began work there in the fall of 1939 and stayed until the following spring when the Hudrliks moved into a new home. Next Dorothy worked for Otto Nelson, a local attorney, and his wife, who preferred a more formal lifestyle. Dorothy served dinner to the couple in the dining room and she ate with the children in the kitchen. Dorothy recalled receiving her weekly pay while she was washing dishes. Mr. Nelson would put the seven dollars on the windowsill. In spite of what seemed like a small wage, Dorothy was still able to put some of the money in the bank.

Like any twenty-year-old, Dorothy wanted to see more of the world. She next ventured to Minneapolis, where she worked for about four months. She doesn't remember what her employer did for a living, but Dorothy recalled ironing many white shirts with a mangle. He must have been in the professional or business world. The Minneapolis houses seemed close together to Dorothy and she remembered riding the bus downtown to shop and see the sights.

In the meantime, Dorothy and John had started dating. On their first date, they went to eat at Costa's in Owatonna, a popular restaurant still located on Cedar Street. They had steak and then drove to Blooming Prairie for the Fourth of July fireworks and a dance. They had been dating for a while before she went to Minneapolis, and they continued to keep in touch by letter. Dorothy rode the bus once to Faribault so she and John could spend time together. Eventually, she decided to return to Owatonna to be closer to John.

Dorothy's final position was with the Lindekugels who owned a Chevrolet dealership in Owatonna. They lived on South Grove Street with their son and daughter. Dorothy enjoyed family breakfasts with the Lindekugels. Mr. Lindekugel occasionally went on hunting trips to South Dakota and brought back game. Once, Dorothy cooked John a dinner of what she thought was one of Mr. Lindekugel's pheasants; much to her embarrassment it turned out to be chicken instead! The Lindekugels appreciated Dorothy's pie baking skills and so did some of the next-door neighbors. It was at the Lindekugel's home that Dorothy had an appendicitis attack and had to have surgery in the Owatonna Hospital. Her father, Frank, paid her medical bills.

John gave Dorothy her engagement ring on her twenty-first birthday while she was working for the Lindekugel family. That fall Dorothy loaned John $150 to purchase a used tractor so that he could get the harvest and plowing done.

3

Vows and a New Family

Wedding Bells for John F. Hondl and Dorothy S. Spindler

John and Dorothy were married in Sacred Heart Catholic Church, Owatonna, Minnesota, on November 26, 1941. It was a morning wedding as were most Catholic weddings in those days. The attendants were Dorothy's niece, Irene Kubista; John's cousin, Elaine Haubenschild; John's friend, Donald Klemmenson; and John's nephew, Donald Ressler.

John and Dorothy made a handsome couple. John, with his dark hair, stood five feet seven inches, just an inch taller than his Grandpa John Haubenschild. He wore a grayish blue suit, most likely purchased for the occasion. Dorothy was just a few inches shorter at five feet four inches tall. Her soft brown curls rimmed her face underneath a veil attached to a seed pearl tiara. The veil was made of bridal illusion fabric and trimmed in Chantilly lace. Dorothy's dress was ivory satin Velveray fashioned in a princess style with a sweetheart neckline and long sleeves fitted to the wrist. The back featured a train and long row of satin covered buttons. Dorothy bought the dress in Mankato, Minnesota, and said it was quite a coincidence that her daughter Colleen also purchased her wedding dress in Mankato, thirty-seven years later. Dorothy also wore a double strand of pearls and carried an arm bouquet of white roses adorned with wide satin ribbon. Her maid of honor, Irene Kubista, wore a blue princess style dress and her attendant, Elaine Haubenschild, wore a similar dress but in pink. Orchids and white chrysanthemums were used to decorate the church.

After the ceremony, close friends and family were invited to a dinner at the farm home belonging to Dorothy's brother John and his wife Sylvia. This was the family home where Dorothy grew up, located three miles east of the village of Pratt. John's family home was on a farm three miles south of Pratt. It is interesting to note that even though these two young people lived only six miles apart, Dorothy said she had never known of the Hondl family until she met John. How communication and transportation advances have changed the likelihood of that occurring today.

John and Dorothy Hondl on the Spindler farm following their wedding, 1941.

It must have been a rare warm sunny day for the late November wedding because Dorothy has photos of the wedding party posing for pictures outdoors standing on the flatbed of a hay wagon. Some guests stayed for supper at John and Sylvia's home and then they joined dozens of friends, relatives and neighbors for a big wedding dance at the Monterey Ballroom, south of Owatonna. The Armand Reazak Band, a very popular band in the area, played polkas, the schottische, which was a partner dance originating in Bohemia, and probably some waltzes.

Bridal party poses on hay wagon at Spindler farm.
From left: Elaine Haubenschild, Irene Kubista, Dorothy, John, Donald Klemmenson, Donald Ressler.

Guests celebrate John and Dorothy's wedding with a group photo on the Spindler farm.

John and Dorothy spent their first night at the Hotel Owatonna. They then took a wedding trip to Michigan City, Indiana, on Lake Michigan, where Dorothy's older cousin Audrey Gilbert lived. John had recently taught Dorothy how to drive, and she did most of the driving on their trip. This set a precedent because Dorothy continued to be the chief "driver" throughout their marriage. In those days, one did not have to take driver training or even pass a test to get a driver's license. Although John did some driving later on, mainly the big livestock truck, he was generally not comfortable behind the wheel because the sight in his left eye was limited. The condition may have been a "lazy eye," that was never recognized or treated in childhood. The left-eye problem, however, did not prevent him from effectively operating machinery or plowing a straight furrow or spotting a weed that needed to be pulled.

John with his new DeSoto on honeymoon trip to Michigan City, Indiana, 1941.

Dorothy said she did not remember much about Michigan City except that it was cool and foggy off the pier on the lake, not surprising in late November. Dorothy recalled that John's mother told the young couple to "hurry back." Over the years, John often used that phrase himself when sending Dorothy or other family members to town for groceries or machinery parts. John usually needed things in a hurry! He was not one to waste time; he knew the importance of taking advantage of good weather and conditions when they were available.

After John and Dorothy returned from their honeymoon, Dorothy's first employer, the Hudrliks, gave them a generous gift. Mr. Hudrlik took Dorothy to Minneapolis via train on a furniture-buying trip enabling her to acquire some quality pieces at discounted wholesale price. Dorothy returned home with a large blond wood dining table with eight chairs and a matching buffet. For the living room she chose a burgundy horsehair type sofa and matching club chair, plus an occasional chair, sofa tables, floor lamp and a blue floral wool area rug. The rug proved to be durable and versatile. It later traveled out of the house with Colleen, who used it in bedrooms in two different homes. Eventually it came back to the Hondl farm and, despite a little bit of wear and fading, it is still in use today by the farmhouse renters.

Serving His Country at Home

Eleven days after John and Dorothy's wedding, the Japanese attack on Pearl Harbor occurred, and several months later the United States was fully engaged in World War II. Like all men between the ages of twenty-one and forty-five, John had to register with the local draft board as required by the United States Selective Service Act of 1940. John's occupation as a farmer was the key factor that kept him out of World War II. Dorothy recalled that when John appeared before the local draft board, he was told that farmers were critically needed at home for food production, and since John was working a large farm on shares with his father, he would be most useful continuing in that role. John was very thankful he did not have to go into the armed services. Like other Americans, John supported the war effort through war bond purchases and making do with shortages imposed by rationing.

Government rationing affected both field work and domestic life on the farm. Even though farmers were expected to produce their best yields for the war effort, Dorothy recalled that permits were required to purchase all tires, new machinery and some machinery parts. When John needed a new hay loader, he was not allowed to purchase one during the war. In the home, meat and sugar were the main foodstuffs rationed with stamps. Dorothy recalled substituting white syrup for sugar when she canned fruit. Meat stamps were not as critical for farm families because they were allowed to butcher some of their own livestock for home use.

Townspeople were not so fortunate. Dorothy remembered giving or trading some of her family's meat ration stamps to friends from town when their allotment for the month was gone.

Starting Married Life

Ordinarily, the start of married life means establishing a new home as a couple. Sometimes there are exceptions. For example, when Dorothy's brother John married, his father remained at the home farm and lived with the young couple. For John and Dorothy, starting married life meant including Clement, one of Dad's older brothers. Clement, who showed signs of depression and mental illness as a young adult, was supposed to move to Owatonna to live with his parents after they rented the farm on shares to John. But John soon realized that Clement would never accept a life "in town" and would probably end up in an institution. Clement lived in his own private world, talking and laughing to himself. He seldom spoke to others and sometimes showed reckless behavior. John was ahead of his time in recognizing that the mentally ill need regular activity and familiar surroundings in order to have any chance at a decent quality of life. He stepped up and did the right thing, offering Clement a place to live and work on the farm where he had grown up.

It must have been difficult when Dorothy arrived at the farm as a young bride and Clement was already a part of the household. After some initial fears and reservations, Dorothy said she accepted the situation and supported John in his decision over the years. Clement worked alongside John and Dorothy as they milked cows by hand and planted and harvested their first crops together. Clement did not always follow John's instructions, sometimes causing damage to property, but for the most part he was able to complete chores and the farm work he was familiar with.

In addition to running the household and helping with outdoor chores, Dorothy quickly jumped into the business side of farming, putting her math and reading skills to good use. While she and John collaboratively made business decisions, Dorothy kept the records, paid the bills and was the negotiator who went to the banks, the accountant and the courthouse, as needed. Dorothy probably knew nearly as much about the farming operation as John, including when machinery purchases were made, which crop varieties were planted and what the commodity prices were at a given time. As part of the noon meal, the

Hondls always had the radio on, listening to the farm market report, which started with prices for prime steers and heifers, went on to slaughter cows, hogs and finally sheep and lambs. The family members were shushed until hog prices were announced, then conversation could resume.

The Girls Arrive

John married Dorothy when he was twenty-eight, an age he felt was late in getting a start on independence and raising a family. As mentioned earlier, his father Anton also was twenty-eight when he married, but that delay may have been related to the three years he spent working in California. In the early 1940s it was probably more typical of young men to marry at age twenty-one or shortly thereafter. John's younger brother George already had been married for more than four years before John and Dorothy walked down the aisle. Dorothy was twenty-one at her wedding and was just as eager as John to start their family.

Nadine, 1943   Bernadette, 1944   Colleen, 1951

Nadine was born on January 4, 1943, in Owatonna Hospital. A few days later, it took the neighborhood's help to bring her and Dorothy home to the farm. It was an extreme winter, with the ditches piled high with snow and township roads nearly impassable. John and a neighbor, Leonard Klecker, brought John's car down to the corner, which was about a mile and a half north of the farm. The county road there was maintained and plowed out more frequently during the winter. They also brought a team of horses. Leonard and the horses stayed at the home of another neighbor, Clarence Homuth, while John drove to pick up

Dorothy and Nadine from the hospital, about nine miles away. When they arrived back at the corner, John had to hitch the horses to the car and pull it the rest of the way in order to get his precious passengers home through the deep snow.

Bernadette arrived in the heat of summer on August 13, 1944, in the midst of the grain harvest. Looking back, Dorothy said she was glad she had the typical eight-to-ten-day stay in the hospital with her new baby because it helped her be ready to get back into the farm routine quickly. In fact, the threshers were at the Hondl farm the day she arrived home with Bernadette. A close relative, Evelyn Soufal, came to help her prepare the noon meal and her sister Roselyn Schrom baked prune and poppy seed filled biscuits for the occasion. Dorothy remembered paying Roselyn for the biscuits, which had taken a lot of time and effort to prepare.

Reflecting on her experience with the threshers' meals, Dorothy recalled that "some neighbors got very competitive." She added that "each family tried to outdo the other in the variety and amount of home-cooked food served." Surely the men in the threshing crew had no complaints about that! The threshing rings were small groups of neighbors and/or relatives who shared manpower and machinery to help each member cost effectively complete his harvest each summer. A threshing machine would be set up in one farmyard; men with teams of horses and wagons would haul the dried grain bundles from the field to the thresher, which separated the grain and the straw. When the next crew member's grain was ripe, the threshing machine and men moved on to the next location.

Colleen was born on June 24, 1951, and was welcomed home by her parents as well as her two older sisters. "Nadine and Bernadette were so proud and excited to have a baby sister," Dorothy reminisced. The two girls stayed with Dorothy's sister-in-law Bertha and her family during the time Dorothy was in the hospital with Colleen. Dorothy remembered that nursing Colleen for the first few months became a real challenge when she had to help with cutting grain at harvest time. The car was brought out to the field so that Nadine and Bernadette could keep an eye on baby Colleen. Dorothy sat in the car and nursed Colleen between rounds when needed. Bernadette recalled that Colleen's birthday celebrations always took place at a beautiful time on the farm – with peonies blossoming on the newly mowed front lawn, crops emerging from the soil and strawberries in season for birthday cake and ice cream.

Working "in town," Dorothy had learned how city folks lived and was certainly influenced by her experiences with the different families. As she raised her own family, Dorothy incorporated some of these entertaining and decorating ideas on the farm. For holidays, the Hondls liked to set a fancy table using white tablecloths and polished silverware and make decorations and centerpieces. With three daughters in the family, they were continually trying new recipes and finding ways to make food look attractive -- *when they had time that is*. The girls enjoyed redecorating their rooms, rearranging the living-room furniture and making curtains. They did a lot of "fussing" as John called it.

4

Farming with Horsepower

John loved horses all of his life, starting with good experiences riding and working with horses as he grew up. He was especially proud of a bronco that he rode back and forth between the home place and a nearby farm, which was eventually owned by his brother George. Horses supplied at least some of the power on the Hondl farm until 1964. John was possibly one of the last farmers in the area to use horses for fieldwork.

At one time, as many as six teams of Belgians and Percherons were stabled in the west wing of the big white barn that anchored the building site. They pulled wagons, sleds, plows and mowers as well as powered the threshing machines in the early years before steam engines. Horses could only make three rounds on the binder, which cut the grain and tied the stems into small bundles. The horses were watered every round. It was such hard work that the horses then had to be rested and replaced, according to John.

On the weekends, the horses went to the pasture and were rounded up on Monday morning for another week of work. John said he never pushed a horse too far in the heat and he never had one drop from exhaustion or overheating. He was also sensitive to problems the horses might be having; he would run his hands over shoulder muscles or pick up a hoof to examine it if the horse seemed to be limping. He routinely cleaned the horses' hooves and trimmed them with a large hoof-trimming tool. He had a talent for knowing what the horses needed.

John recollected how sleeping sickness affected his family's horses. In 1938 sleeping sickness or equine encephalitis infected the horses at threshing time in the Midwest. The epidemic was somewhat unusual in that the disease was more common in the southern and eastern parts of the United States. It was spread through a bird-to-mosquito-to-horse cycle. It is possible that climate conditions that summer may have contributed to more mosquitoes that led to the spread of the disease.

Equine encephalitis results in fever accompanied by nervous signs including sensitivity to sound, periods of excitement, and restlessness. Brain lesions appear, causing drowsiness, drooping ears, circling, aimless wandering, inability to swallow and abnormal gait. Paralysis follows, causing the horse to have difficulty raising its head. In the United States, 300,000 horses and mules were stricken that year having a major impact on agricultural production.[13] The Hondl horses showed symptoms of little energy, drooping ears and lack of stamina.

John recalled that the veterinarian treated the sick horses by putting ice on the back of the neck to cool the brain. Then the doctor bled them each night by opening a vein in the horse's neck. When the bleeding was finished, he would use the animal's own tail hair to close the wound. The Hondl horses did not die, but they were not strong enough to work after suffering from equine encephalitis. They seemed to have no endurance and were put in the pasture in hopes they might recover completely. Some had to be sold and were replaced with healthy new draft horses. Eventually vaccines prevented further outbreaks of the disease. The Hondls had no reoccurrences of equine encephalitis in the next three decades of using horses on the farm.

John speculated that the disease could possibly have been planned by the government to support the rising machine industry. No matter what caused the epidemic, it contributed to the demise of horsepower and growth of tractor use.

The Horses Most Remembered

Nadine, Bernadette and Colleen recalled a number of teams on the farm. There was the team of Dick and Florrie, which replaced a team of grays. These roans were purchased from Earl McNerney who lived a few miles south of the Hondl farm. Instead of loading them up, John walked them home. Dick was a challenge to *feed* as he would try to bite, to *harness* as he would crowd John against the side of the stall and to *drive* as he would exercise a mind of his own. Uncle Clement drove the team of chestnuts, Bud and Cub. One of the chestnuts died and was replaced by a Belgian mare named Kate. She was very skinny when she came to the Hondl farm after John purchased her; he said Kate could not get enough to eat for several months. She just ate and ate and ate.

Colleen on Bud, one of the Hondl draft horses.

John prepares to load Juney and Victor, two riding horses born on the farm, 1950s.

Since John loved horses, the family owned more than just the workhorses. There were many trips to West Concord, Minnesota to visit a horse trader who turned up some riding horses for the girls. Nadine and

Bernadette rode Daisy, who eventually produced Juney and Victor. On Sunday afternoons in the winter, Daisy would be enlisted to pull one of the girls on a small sled or skis on the field road to the east, turn around in a small clearing and then head back home.

Colleen loved the horses as much as her father. She never got to drive the teams, but John let her hold the reins. In the quest to get Colleen a riding horse, a Shetland pony named Trigger was purchased at the sales barn in Albert Lea, Minnesota. He was well behaved for about a month and then he became mean, biting and kicking anyone who came near. John thought Trigger had been drugged. Eventually, John purchased a twelve-year-old black Morgan mare named Bess at a sales barn near Lakeville, Minnesota. She turned out to be a wonderful horse. Colleen remembered great times when she rode Bess to herd and count the beef cows and their calves in the pasture. Bess had worked with cattle before and knew just what to do. Colleen liked having her friend Theresa Nass from Owatonna come out to the farm to ride on the grassy field roads. The day would start with grooming Kate and Bess, brushing their coats until they shone, combing their manes and tails, and sometimes braiding in a few ribbons for fun. The girls even tried setting up small "jumps" about a foot high on the grassy field road. Kate simply ignored the jump trotting right through it, but Bess actually jumped thrilling the girls.

End of an Era

At one time horses pulled just about everything from manure spreaders, plows, cultivators and mowers, to corn wagons, corn pickers and grain binders. Hauling manure was the last task the horses performed on the Hondl farm. Uncle Clement often did this job. He would pitch manure by hand from the horse or cattle barns onto a flat hayrack and drive the load to the field where he pitched it off by hand. He seemed to enjoy the work, doing it nearly year around. By 1964, there was no machinery to hitch the horses to anymore. John kept the two teams for a while, but eventually the last of his beloved workhorses had to be sold. No doubt this was sad for him as the horses had worked hard and had been a part of farm life for many years. Bess stayed around for a few more years, which may have helped fill the void. She died at the age of twenty-five, a good, long life for a horse.

5

Good Help Was Hard To Get

With modern machinery being quite expensive, manpower continued to be vital to successful farming. In the 1940s, if an individual family was not large enough to plant or bring in the harvest, the farmer would rely on various sources of help including carnival workers, the Office of Employment and even German prisoners of war.

Dorothy remembered carnival workers, who were big and strong and also carried daggers, coming to work on the farm; they were not the safest folks to have around young children. The Hondls were fortunate and had no bad incidents. The carnival workers who were looking for ways to earn extra money were hired through the local Office of Employment. John usually employed two workers; sometimes they stayed at the farm for several days at a time, depending on the work needed.

During the summer of 1945, German prisoners of war (POWs) helped with the threshing and grain harvest on the Hondl farm. Earlier that year a POW camp had been set up on the Cashman farm, near the intersection of County Road 45 and 26th Street in the north part of present day Owatonna. The camp initially held thirty-five prisoners but that number rose as high as 300 during the next two years.[14] Dorothy recalled that John would drive to the camp early in the morning to pick up two POWs for each workday. John spoke some German and so did his father, so communication did not seem to be a problem. Probably show-and-tell was all that was needed to give instructions for loading bundles, pitching them into the threshing machine and stacking the straw. The POWs had to be returned on time. One evening the threshing crew worked past dark, prompting the camp administrator to call the Hondls to ask why the prisoners had not been returned. Minnesota ran seventeen camps, using the prisoners mainly for harvest labor, food processing and logging. Prisoners were not allowed to practice any trade they may have been trained for but could pursue hobbies and art interests when they were not working.

In one incident involving other temporary employees, Dorothy's wedding ring was stolen. The workers had been in the house for breakfast and must have seen Dorothy take off her ring and put it in an empty cream pitcher while she washed dishes. When Dorothy told John the ring was missing, he spoke to all the workers and said no questions would be asked if they would just return the ring. So, within the next couple of days, the ring turned up in a full pitcher of cream. Dorothy still wears the ring to this day.

Workers were treated as fairly and humanely as possible. When they arrived, John regularly asked the men if they had eaten breakfast. If they had not, Dorothy was called upon to "rustle up some grub" – in a hurry of course. Since eggs and bread were plentiful and a side of bacon was usually hanging in the pantry, breakfast was an easy meal to serve in short order. Workers also enjoyed a major meal at noon: roast beef or pork, mashed potatoes, vegetables from the garden and, for sure, a dessert of pie or fruit cobbler if there wasn't enough time to make pies. Afternoon lunches also were served to keep workers going until dark when necessary. Workers consumed baloney sandwiches, lemonade and cookies or bars under the shade of a tree or the barn or even out in the field in the shadow of a tractor wheel.

6

The Least Favorite Season - Making Hay

Haying season was one of the busiest times on the farm for the Hondls and for the horses. Up through the late 1950s, horses hitched to a mower did the hay cutting. Nadine and Bernadette both grew up learning how to drive horses. One job was driving a team hitched to a hayrack and pulling a hay loader behind. John or Uncle Clement would stack the hay neatly in the hayrack, filling up three slings. The challenge was to drive so the row of hay stayed right between the two horses with the wagon pole straddling the middle of the hay row. The girls always hated coming to the end of the row and having to turn back into the next one to get the team, hayrack and hay loader properly lined up. Somehow lots of itchy hay and dust found its way down the backs of their shirts as the stackers threw the loose hay up to the front of the hayrack. As the hay piled up, the driver had to straddle the wagon ladder at higher levels to stay above the hay and see well enough to drive the horses.

Unloading the big hayracks of loose hay required the entire family's help. While kids today learn teamwork by playing sports, the Hondl daughters learned it by putting hay in the barn. Here's how it worked. Whoever was at home scanned the field road to watch for the arrival of the loads pulled by the teams of horses. That person helped the load driver park close to the barn and then placed wooden blocks behind and in front of the wagon tires to keep it from rolling out of place. An elaborate towrope and pulley system raised the slings of hay from the hayrack to the hayloft door at the top of the barn. The youngest family members contributed by pulling back the large towrope after a tractor (usually driven by Dorothy) pulled the rope about 100 yards. The daughters remembered swallowing a lot of dust and developing arm muscles from that job. Kids also helped with the signaling. John would be up in the hayloft and would yell "dump it" and Clement would trip the rope to unleash the sling of hay. Then one of the girls would use hand signals to tell the towrope tractor driver to stop backing up and return.

Finally, they would drag the rope back and start all over again. If things went well, the family could unload a wagon in about twenty or thirty minutes. Up in the hot hayloft, John and his lucky co-worker used forks to spread the hay to the edges of the barn walls to keep the pile level.

After they got two or three wagons unloaded, the family would have lunch in the shade of the silos where, hopefully a nice breeze would cool them off on a sticky July afternoon. Lemonade or Kool-Aid, baloney sandwiches, some type of homemade cookies or brownies refueled everyone so they could go back out to the prairie for three more loads before dark.

Everyone contributed to get this big job done; even the youngest family members would "help" any way they could. In one example Colleen remembered that when she was about five or six, she was supposed to "help" her dad in the hayloft

John and a team of horses bring a large load of hay from the prairie to the farm site, late 1940s.

with spreading the loose hay. It was probably more to keep him company than anything else. One job she could handle at that age was climbing the ladder with a fruit jar filled with cold water for whoever was working in the hot and dusty hayloft.

Battling the Back Prairie

The "prairie" was the most distant field from the home place. Making the hay there often presented a challenge. Big ruts in the wet spongy peat ground where the Hondls had gotten stuck in previous years might hold water or upset a wagonload of hay. Dorothy side-raked the hay, which meant turning it over so it would dry better. The side-rake also rolled several swaths together to enable the hay baler to pick up the hay more efficiently. Nobody enjoyed this job because John wanted the rows just so and the hay sometimes had a mind of its own. With practice, however, Dorothy got to be good at it, and the job eventually went faster when a tractor was used. Bernadette and Nadine were thrilled they never had to learn this skill, but Colleen was lucky enough to acquire expertise in side raking. That expertise did not come easily; one time John yelled at Colleen when she didn't do the side-raking correctly. In frustration, Colleen got off the tractor and walked the half-mile home. Her father's occasionally short temper combined with the challenge of getting the hay into the barn before it rained sometimes made for tense times.

New Techniques, New Challenges

Gradually the haymaking system changed. John bought a mower pulled by a tractor. In time, the Hondls cut hay with a swather, sometimes operated by Colleen. The purchase of a hay baler eliminated the hauling

A grain elevator is used to raise bales to the top of a large straw stack, 1972.

of loose hay. Bales were stacked on wagons to be brought home to the barn. In the minds of the three Hondl girls, the baler made huge bales; they always seemed much heavier than they should have been to handle easily, especially the alfalfa hay.

John and the family had a love-hate relationship with the baler; it definitely saved labor but at times could be challenging to operate. There was a shearing pin system built in that actually prevented the baler from taking in too much hay. The metal pin would "shear off" and the whole system would shut down. The excess hay would have to be pulled out and re-distributed in the swaths. Shearing a pin was a good thing on one hand, but on the other hand it caused delays and frustration, especially when the supply of extra pins ran out.

In addition, the baler had a large enclosed container in back for four spools of twine. It was very important to never let the twine run out as it was tedious to thread it back through the machine. There was a trick to connecting the twine from the bottom spool to the top; it had to be done just right and John had the gift.

Haymaking also changed with raising alfalfa. For some time, most of the forage on the Hondl farm was grass hay from the prairie. Later, John began to grow alfalfa, which had to be carefully planted and harvested at the right time. Alfalfa contained more protein as needed by a changing livestock production system.

The methods of collecting the hay and getting it into the hay barn also evolved. For a few years, a flatbed was pulled behind a tractor, and one person on each side lifted up the bales from the field and stacked them on the flatbed. The next improvement involved pulling the flatbed directly behind the baler so the person on the flatbed could stack them right as they came out of the baler. For a time, bales were put into slings similar to the loose hay. Eventually, slings gave way to stacking them directly on the flatbed. The bales were unloaded individually onto a conveyor that was connected to a track at the top of the barn. A device on the track could be switched to direct the bales to either side so the hayloft stackers did not have to carry them as far. The conveyor made unloading faster and used a little less manpower and Hondl girl power.

Straw Was Easy

Similar methods were used for straw bales. It was almost fun to work with straw bales because they were so much lighter and easier to handle than the alfalfa bales. There was an old straw shed that stood next to the granary. In between loads as the straw shed was being filled, young Colleen would imagine it as a house inviting the cats and family dog in to play.

Straw and hay bales also were piled into huge outdoor stacks. In earlier times when pigs were put out in a small field, their housing was made out of loose straw stacked over a wooden structure. Later on, bales were used instead. Either way made for a nice warm place for the pigs in the winter.

7

Getting Up to Speed with Machinery

Like other farmers, John and his father evolved by using a combination of horses and tractors to get the work done. John bought his first row crop tractor with a cultivator for between $1,000 and $1,200 in 1942. He was probably inspired by his brother George, who bought a John Deere tractor and planter in 1938 and was able to farm his entire 160 acres with just one team and a row crop tractor. It was a smaller farm, but nevertheless the tractor power made a huge difference.

Although John loved his four-legged horsepower, he recognized the value of buying the latest machinery to get crops planted and harvested efficiently. In 1948, he was the first in Steele County to purchase a set of Goodyear Super-Grip tractor tires. The *Steele County Photo News* featured John and his new tire purchase in the January 8, 1948, issue.

——— The Steele County Photo News, Owatonna, Minnesota, Thur:
Goodyear Tires Go Through

Getting through 100 acres of wet, soggy, muggy, tough-to-whip soil was finally accomplished for John Hondl, operating more than 400 acres on route 5, this week when he got the first set of Goodyear new Super-Grip tractor tires in the county.

The installation was made by Wanous Tire and Battery, local Goodyear dealers, and Hondl probably rides on the largest set of tires in the county when he takes this one tractor out. Here Mr. Hondl is shown looking over the deep tread and cleaning features of the tire.

The Sure-Grips are 15 inches in diameter and run well over five feet in height. Designed to bite through all kinds of mud and difficult soil, the tire is constructed with a cut in the high tread which provides a self-cleaning feature.

"Mud just won't lodge in this tire," Wanous declared, "and the Sure-Grips go through soil conditions that farmers have never been able to work before because they couldn't get a tractor through certain acreages."

Mr. Hondl is a confined (confirmed) Goodyear tire user, according to Mr. Wanous, having Goodyear sets on both tractors and a repeat buyer. [15]

The Only Combine the Hondls Ever Had

Later, in 1951, John and Dorothy purchased what was then only the third combine to be used in Steele County. The cost was $5,400, some of which was borrowed from Security Bank and Trust Company in Owatonna. Typical of those with Czech and German heritage, John and Dorothy could not get that loan paid off soon enough. The combine was stored in a building at the Steele County fairgrounds until it was ready to be used. Relatives were surprised by the purchase, and they had been wondering why John had not made arrangements to be part of the regular neighborhood threshing ring. John was not one to brag or let other people know of his plans. He made his own decisions, based on reading farm publications, anticipating trends and trusting Dorothy's good judgment. Farming still involves risks every season, especially when the farmer has to borrow money for machinery and supplies that may or may not produce crops with sufficient profits to pay back loans. Most of John's long-term decisions proved to be wise investments and so the farm thrived.

John on his beloved Massey-Harris 27 combine, 1951. The combine replaced the threshing machine reducing manual labor involved in the grain harvest.

The Massey-Harris 27 combine was John's pride and joy and, even after it outlived its usefulness, John had a soft spot in his heart for the machine. Its final resting place was in the oak woods north of the farmyard. That machine helped John harvest thousands of bushels of soybeans, oats and wheat over the years. It was not the easiest machine to operate. One summer John had a bad back and he could not step the combine clutch without extreme pain. So Bernadette became an assistant operator, riding the combine and stepping the clutch at the appropriate times, while John steered and ran the reel, brake, throttle and all other aspects of the machine. Somehow, they got the oats crop harvested that summer. Combining was hot, dusty, boring work. At the end of the day, John would be covered in black dust. Sometimes he would clean up first before coming in the house, using a washbasin placed outdoors on a milk can by the old porch. Lots of Lava soap was used every summer.

In later years, John studied the new Massey-Harris combine brochures and visited numerous farm implement dealers thinking maybe it was time to replace his beloved M-H 27. Even his granddaughter Sara Thomasy knew that her Grandpa Hondl longed for a new combine; she always said that someday she would buy him one. It turns out one was never needed. John hired other farmers and neighbors with larger more up-to-date machines to combine his crops for him.

Dorothy the Grain Hauler

Over the years, Dorothy made hundreds of trips with the Dodge livestock and grain truck delivering wheat and soybeans to sell at various grain elevators in the area. She was well known to the elevator operators and could handle the loaded truck like a pro, pulling a full grain box behind. Nadine, Bernadette and Colleen would accompany her on some of these trips; sometimes it yielded a candy bar or bag of peanuts as a treat. Years later, Sara and Clare, two of Dorothy's granddaughters, also had fond memories of riding in the big red truck with their Grandma Hondl at the wheel. It was exciting for the youngsters to sit up high in the truck cab and feel like they were grownups doing an important job; Grandma loved their company, too.

Dorothy and granddaughter Clare Thomasy are ready to take a load of wheat to the elevator, 1988.

Dorothy told one story that made her consider quitting her job as the grain hauler. She was taking soybeans to the elevator late in the day. She had the big truck loaded and also was pulling a full grain box behind the truck. She drove to the Hope, Minnesota elevator, but they could not take the beans. So, she called John and asked what to do. He said to go to Clark's Grove just a few miles away. In the meantime, John and the hired man helped themselves to the pork chop supper Dorothy had prepared.

She successfully got the soybeans unloaded at Clark's Grove and arrived home thinking she would finally get to eat. But, there was no pork chop left for her as the hired man had eaten more than his share. Dorothy was ready to make the guys wash the dishes!

8

The Main Enterprise
Takes a New Direction

Throughout the 1940s, John and Dorothy had a herd of about twenty-five milk cows. The cows were stanchioned in two rows facing outward with a center aisle in between. There were two milk machines, which Dorothy operated. They were placed on a cart that was pushed along the center aisle. At first, with no electricity, the machines were powered by a gas engine. In 1947, electricity was installed in the house, chicken coop and barn making milking and other chores much easier. The milk went from the machine's container to cans, which were placed into a tank where cold flowing well water cooled the milk. The milk cans were loaded up daily and hauled to the Pratt Creamery. Here was yet another opportunity for a treat for Nadine and Bernadette when they rode along.

The cows, as Dorothy discovered, definitely had individual personalities. Some never got used to the milk machine and had to be milked by hand. Cows were also creatures of habit. Dorothy recalled one time when she went on the wrong side of one of the cows; it started kicking immediately.

In 1951, John and Dorothy surprised their relatives and neighbors with their decision to get out of the dairy business. John had had enough of the tedious and demanding work of milking cows. There was also an opportune time to make a change. On the estate auction after his mother died, John sold his share of the cows and did not bid on the others. This gave him a small stake with which to start a beef operation, perhaps inspired by his Uncle Paul Haubenschild in Montana. John and Dorothy bought their first herd of white-face heifers from Canada.

This decision was a major departure given that most farmers in Steele County had dairy herds. In fact, Steele County was known from 1898 to 1940 as the "Butter Capitol of the World." Switching from dairy to beef production was going against common practice as evidenced by the 1951 Annual Report of the Southeastern Minnesota Farm Management Service.

Out of 169 farms covering fourteen counties, only nine had beef breeding herds.[16]

Over the next fifteen years, John was continually on the lookout for more calves for the next year's group of feeder cattle. This quest for cattle led to literally hundreds of buying excursions throughout Minnesota, North and South Dakota, Nebraska and even Montana. Following established habits, Dorothy was the driver for most of these trips. Although that was a lot of time on the road, it got John and Dorothy off the farm and out to see new territory. John also had his favorite sales barns and breeders.

John's ultimate goal was to have his own beef cows so that he would not have to buy yearling calves because he was never sure what he was getting. He hit the jackpot in 1965 in Mapleton, Minnesota, with some Black Angus heifers that each produced a dozen or more calves over the years. Colleen recalled the spring they had the first crop of calves. She was about fifteen years old and remembered having to go out to the barnyard frequently to check the cows to see if any were about to start calving. Typically the calving season stretched from late March to mid-June. John and Dorothy often did night duty as sometimes the cows chose nighttime to deliver.

On the Road to South St. Paul

Selling the beef cattle was a tense and sometimes challenging last step in the family's beef business. Weeks before, John would listen to the radio at noon to catch the markets, trying to pick a good time to sell. It was always a gamble and could determine how much, if any, profits were made. In the 1950s most of the Hondl cattle went to South Saint Paul, where a variety of commission firms kept the stock and tried to sell them for the best price to one of the three or four packing companies. John, like many cattle raisers, distrusted the "commission men" because there was no way to be sure they obtained the best price per pound or if someone had tampered with the scales. Also, for a two or three-cent per pound commission, it seemed like they got a nice check for little work.

The day before taking cattle to St. Paul, the family would put the racks up on the red Dodge livestock and grain truck and fill the gas tank. Sometimes they would sort out the ten or eleven head of cattle they wanted to sell and keep them separate. On selling day, everyone in the family got up at 4:00 A.M. to help load the cattle, a nerve-wracking job that nobody liked. John backed the truck up to the bullpen door and Dorothy and the girls helped herd the cattle on the truck. Sometimes the cattle were skittish, and the family had to be careful so the animals did not slip and break a leg or become injured.

Nadine or Bernadette often rode with John to South St. Paul. Sometimes Dorothy went too, accompanied by Colleen before she was in school. Two heads were better than one on the drive, for navigating the streets and for collecting the check. It was about a three-hour one-way trip in the truck and ideally John would be unloading in South St. Paul by 8:00 or 8:30 A.M. The cattle would be driven to one of hundreds of pens in the stockyards. There were walkways high above the pens and alleys allowing quick access to the entire stockyard.

Buyers represented the various commission firms. They were the ones who evaluated the cattle and offered a bid. John and whoever accompanied him went to one of the small "warming" houses where they would wait for the buyers to come back with their offers. It was definitely a man's world in the warming houses. Often times the walls would be covered with risqué pictures and calendars, which were quite shocking and embarrassing to the Hondl girls. Very few women, let alone young girls, visited the stockyards in those days.

Next, the Hondls would walk to the Hook'Em Cow Restaurant for breakfast. Nadine and Bernadette remembered feeling out-of-place in the crowd of loud truckers and stockyard men, but any breakfast in a restaurant was a rare treat and to be enjoyed. Then the girls and their dad returned to the stockyards to sit in the little shack, reading old magazines and trying to keep warm, while the commission salesmen walked around with their whips, working to sell the cattle to the highest bidder. Hopefully, the cattle would sell before noon. John always thought the earlier the stock sold, the better the price and the earlier he could get going home. Once the cattle were sold, the owner went to the Livestock Exchange Building a few blocks away to pick up the check. John was happy to get his check while the daughters enjoyed the free items given out, including bullet pencils, plastic piggy banks and little notebooks advertising the James T. Crosby and Sons, Security and Bennett Commission Companies.

The first group of Black Angus calves the Hondls raised, 1967.

A partitioned wood fence allows calves to get their feed ration
in the barnyard, while cows remain in the woods, 1967.

One year there were more cattle than normal ready for market within
a period of roughly two weeks. John had taken several loads to South St.
Paul during this time accompanied on the last trip by Bernadette. On the
trip home, the Minnesota Highway Patrol stopped them. The officers

thought John was hauling cattle for others – without a commercial license. John was able to prove that these cattle were from his own herd and that he was not hauling other people's stock.

If all went according to schedule, the Hondls would be back in Owatonna in time for Bernadette and Nadine to go to school for a few hours. Their dad would pull up in the big red cattle truck in front of St. Mary's School on South Cedar Street and drop them off. Bernadette and Nadine would pray that none of their classmates was looking out the window to see them getting out of the big smelly livestock truck. Although the girls worried about having cattle odor on their clothes, they did not recall ever being teased about it. The possibility of being laughed at was probably enough to embarrass them. As farm kids new to a city school, they may have felt like outsiders at times and did not want to do anything to draw negative attention.

John and Rex give family members a farm tour in 1993. The fence built in 1966 was still doing its job, keeping the beef herd in the pasture.

Fencing Them In

In the spring of 1966, the pasture fence had to be rebuilt so that the first group of beef cows and their calves could graze there. Fence making had been done periodically over the years, but this was the biggest project of all. The Hondl family did not especially enjoy fence making. It was boring and tedious, and one never seemed to make much progress. The fence corners and ends were anchored with large wooden posts that were heavy and hard to handle. The holes for each wooden post had to be dug by hand with a posthole auger since John did not have power equipment to do the job. John and Uncle Clement were the only ones strong enough to dig the holes. The steel posts were pounded into the ground with a heavy, metal, tube-shaped tool. That was hard work too. Fence making was dangerous, especially when the woven wire or the top barbwires were being stretched. This had to be done carefully with the tension just right so the wires were taut but not so tight that they would snap. Dorothy recalled one time when she was cut on the upper arm by a wire that broke. One of the easier jobs was attaching clamps to hold the wire to the steel posts; Dorothy and the girls, equipped with pliers and a pail of clamps, handled that task. Bernadette recalled helping her family work on the pasture fence before leaving for her first position teaching English in Port Huron, Michigan. When completed, the pasture fence was a source of pride.

9

More Than Beef

Typically, farms in the mid-1900s raised several different kinds of livestock. In Steele County, it would have been common to have milk cows, pigs and chickens. For the Hondls, it was beef cows, pigs and chickens. John often said that having different kinds of livestock and a variety of crops meant that, if one went bad, the others might make up for it. In other words, there was good reason to diversify.

Pigs, Pigs and More Pigs

John really enjoyed and focused on the beef operation, but he and Dorothy supplemented their income over time   by raising a large number of pigs. Typically they raised two crops of pigs, with spring litters arriving in March and fall litters in September.

Over the years, the sows were kept in different locations on the farm. In the early years, they were taken up to the "willows," a small grove of trees about a quarter mile south of the home place. During the summer, the sows could root around the grove and shelter themselves in a very dusty straw shed. These straw sheds, located in several places on the farm, were made by stacking loose straw or bales on a wooden structure as described earlier. Later, sows were also situated along the field road to the east of the farm place. A tractor was used to pull a wooden feeding platform and a large portable structure for shade and shelter. A grass area would be fenced in for the pigs. Feed and water had to be hauled out to these remote locations. Eventually, to avoid the problem of having to haul water over long distances, John stretched a long, hard black rubber hose out to the pig lot on the east field road.

To service the sows, boars had to be purchased. John usually bought them from Myron Authfather, a farmer who raised and sold purebred Poland China breeding stock near Austin. The Authfather family belonged to the Seventh Day Adventist Church, which observed the Sabbath on Saturday instead of Sunday. As a young child, Colleen could not understand that concept and noted that Myron was always in his work clothes when the Hondl family sometimes visited them on Sunday afternoon drives.

When the sows were farrowing (having their litter of little pigs), they were housed in several different places. For a time, housing was in the large portable structures mentioned earlier. These were put in a convenient spot on the farmyard. Inside the structure, pens were built on both sides with a narrow walkway between the pens. It was tricky to feed the sows as they would jump up with their front feet on the top of the pen. It could be scary and a little dangerous as they were hungry and were also in a mood to protect their litters. In the winter, litters were also raised in pens along the north side of the barn, in the large pen to the west and in the former horse stall area.

Colleen, age four, enjoys petting a silky smooth litter of baby pigs.

When the time came to sell the pigs, the process followed a pattern much like with the beef cattle. The family got up early to load and someone usually rode with John to South St. Paul. In later years, the hogs were sold to George A. Hormel & Company in Austin and Wilson & Company in Albert Lea. Both Minnesota meat packing plants were about an hour drive from the farm.

John the Veterinarian

John had to be a "practicing" veterinarian during much of his farm career. He gave shots and dehorned the beef cattle. When he started the beef herd, John helped the cows deliver their calves when they needed assistance. He also helped sows deliver numerous litters.

One particular task that John took on as did most farmers was castrating pigs. Actually, castrating pigs was more of a family project, one that Dorothy described as "a horrible job." To aid in the process, the girls either handled the gates keeping the pigs in or held the wiggling, squealing young pigs up by their hind legs while John wielded the knife and poured on the antiseptic. Every now and then the job did not get done when it should have maybe in part because it was a highly dreaded task. As a result, the pigs sometimes were much heavier than they should have been and thus more difficult to control. Uncle Clement had to be the one to hold them as the girls could not keep the squirming animals steady enough for the delicate surgery. John was proud to say he had very few pigs develop an infection from the operation.

Although John handled as many veterinary tasks as he could, he called on a "real" veterinarian for serious cases needing a diagnosis. In these cases, John had ultimate faith in Dr. Ralph Myers, who was the Hondls' long-time "real" veterinarian. For example, when John realized that a beef cow or a sow was in trouble delivering its young, he would call Doc Myers, as he was known. Dr. Myers lived in a big white house in Owatonna, where he also had his office. He was Owatonna's first college-educated veterinarian and was a well-respected member of the community and also served as Owatonna's postmaster.[17]

The Chickens and the Eggs

Farmwomen in the 1940s through the early 1960s often took care of chickens. The sale of the eggs provided them with household money to buy groceries and items the family needed. The Hondl farm was no different.

Each year in the early spring, about 500 chicks were purchased. The cuddly, soft, yellow peeping chicks were brought home in large boxes and put in a small movable structure called a brooder house with heat lamps to keep them warm. There were typically some roosters in the mix, which were later butchered and eaten. However, the majority of the 500 were layers, meaning they would lay eggs when they matured. They grew quickly and eventually were moved into the big chicken coop, replacing the previous year's old hens. One of the typical chicken raising practices Dorothy used was to purchase bags of pearly oyster shells. She fed the oyster shells to the chickens when they started producing eggs to provide calcium ensuring a strong eggshell.

The chicken coop was not a pleasant place. First, there was the smell. The manure smell grew stronger as the manure grew deeper. Eventually, Uncle Clement would clean it out and spread the manure on the fields for fertilizer. Second, there were mean chickens. The chickens laid their eggs in little wooden compartments that were about four rows high and attached to the walls of the chicken coop. The mean chickens would make it challenging to pick the eggs they were sitting on from the little compartments without getting pecked. Finally, there were the rats. It was scary to reach into the top compartments since a few rats sometimes inhabited the chicken coop. The girls were afraid that a rat might be sitting up there waiting for them to reach in. Nadine remembered that they would bang on the nest boxes to scare away the vermin.

Though they spent much of their time in the coop, the chickens were sometimes allowed to run loose. Colleen remembered riding her bicycle through the chickens trying to entice the roosters to chase her. Roosters could be mean so she had to ride fast. In the evening, however, all the chickens would voluntarily return to the chicken coop and go up on the roosts. One of the girls would have to run down and lock the door to keep the chickens from going out too early in the morning and also to keep predators, such as a fox or the neighbor's dog, out.

After the eggs were collected, cleaning them was a major chore and was usually done by the daughters. Sometimes eggs would break in the nest making others dirty. Those would have to be soaked in cool water and wiped carefully to get them clean. The clean eggs were placed in layers into a case which held thirty dozen. When a case was full the girls were happy and Dorothy would take it to Owatonna to sell at Kasper's, a local grocery store.

10

Corn, Oats, Wheat and Soybeans

In the mid-1900s, the necessity of farming diversity also extended to crops. A variety of crops was required for feeding and bedding the livestock. Farms needed to be fairly independent, growing as much as possible to meet their own needs. Family farms then were small by today's standards; a quarter section, meaning 160 acres, was typical. The Hondl farm was considered fairly large at 394 acres, even though part of it was pasture and grassland for hay.

Testing the Seeds

One of the staple crops on the farm was corn. As spring approached, John tested his seed corn by placing the kernels in damp cloths in a dish or pan behind the kitchen stove. He laid exactly 100 seeds in the moist pan and then determined the germination percentage by counting the number of seeds that sprouted. Colleen remembered helping count the sprouts, again and again, to make sure the number was correct. The testing was also done with soybean seeds.

Time To Plant, Time To Weed

In the early years, standard crops were corn, wheat, oats and hay. This mid-century crop mix in mid-western United States, which included a variety of small grains, is very similar to present day crops in the Czech Republic.

Over the decades, the corn crop was planted in a variety of ways. In the early years, horses pulled a one or two-row corn planter. After John's father Anton retired, he continued to come out to the farm to do the corn planting with a team of horses and a two-row planter. For a few years, corn was "checked," meaning it was planted in such a way that it could be cultivated in both crosswise directions. A cultivator was used to dig out the weeds and loosen the soil between the rows of corn after they were planted. In order to cultivate the field in both directions without digging out corn plants, the seeds within the rows had to be in an absolutely perfect grid formation.

Later on, a major time-saving improvement was to use a tractor to pull a four-row corn planter. Herbicide use later eliminated the need to "check" the corn but it still had to be cultivated. Dorothy often did the cultivating as she was a very precise driver and was good at not digging out the young corn plants. She went out early in the morning and got a lot done before the girls had even started their day. Eventually corn was planted closer together with more herbicides, thus eliminating the need for cultivation.

Dorothy did not enjoy corn-planting season because she was allergic to the herbicide dust on the seed corn. She had to be careful not to touch or breathe it in. If she did, she would break out in painful blisters on her scalp and face. Sometimes she would cover her nose and mouth with a wet towel for protection. The best thing was to stay away from the treated seed and just let John fill the planter boxes.

Penny a Stem

In spite of using a cultivator and chemical weed control, some undesirable plants still appeared in the Hondl fields. So, the last resort was to pull them by hand. At about age ten, all three daughters earned their first wages by picking weeds in the soybean, corn, wheat and oat fields. Their dad paid a penny a stem for each mustard weed, sow thistle or French weed they brought home. It was an unpleasant, tedious task, but the incentive worked.

The family usually went weed picking mid-morning after their chores. This allowed them to beat the heat but was late enough to avoid getting soaked with the dew. Wearing long-sleeved shirts, jeans and gloves, they drove to the field in the car or by tractor, leaving a jar of cold water in a brown paper bag nearby to quench their thirst. Some of the weeds grew in patches, but even so the girls often had to hop over rows of thigh-high soybeans or go between waist-high corn plants to reach the distant weeds. To locate weeds not yet in blossom, they walked up and down several rows at a time throughout the field. The prickly, sticky sow thistles were difficult to pull and so were the mustard plants that sometimes grew four or five feet tall. The French weed had a nasty odor but was easier to pull. The girls stuffed the weeds into empty concentrate sacks or burlap bags, being careful not to scatter any seed from the blossoms.

After several hours, they were hot and tired from pulling weeds and carrying their now heavier sacks. The ride home felt wonderful. When they got home, the girls carefully counted their weed stems. They are not sure their dad actually cared how accurate they were; he was happy that those weeds were no longer growing in the field. Years later, Colleen suggested that maybe she should have been paid more – inflation rate, at least two cents a stem.

August – Small Grain Harvest

The oats and wheat crops were harvested in mid-summer. Most of the oats was stored in the old granary or the bin above the horse barn and later ground for feed. The Massey-Harris 27 combine, described earlier, separated out the grain from the straw chaff. The combine had a device that in turn, would separate out any weed seeds still mixed in with the grain. The weed seeds all went into a sack, which had to be emptied periodically. The combine did not necessarily separate out the insects. The girls thought it was fascinating to look into the wagonloads of grain and see all kinds of beetles, grasshoppers and crickets, many of them still hopping around.   There was a certain excitement in the air when the combining was underway. As the wagonloads of grain arrived home, the family felt happy and satisfied that their hard work was bringing good results. The best scenario was to complete the grain harvest before the Steele County Fair got underway in the second week of August. That way the girls could focus on their 4-H project entries and the whole family could enjoy the fair.

Silo Filling and Fall Harvest

Some of the corn crop went into the silo for silage to be used as cattle feed. Silo filling, a major task in early to mid-September, began with the Hondls hiring a neighbor to "open up" their fields. To do this, the neighbor used a self-propelled machine to cut down the first rows making room for the Hondls' corn chopper, which was pulled by a tractor. A silage wagon was hooked on behind the chopper. John ran the chopper out in the field and someone else, usually Dorothy or Uncle Clement, brought the full loads back to the home place. If the girls were not in school, they helped unload.

The silage wagon had a movable false-front that pushed the chopped corn along toward the back of the wagon where it was dumped into an auger. The false front was moved along by chains powered by an attachment connected to a tractor's power takeoff system. Once in the auger, the chopped corn was fed into a blower, which then forced the silage up approximately forty feet through the pipes into the silo at the top.

The moisture content of the corn was very important both for corn to be made into silage as well as dry corn described later. Moisture content of the corn plant needed to be at about fifty-five to sixty-five percent at the time of chopping. A hot, dry day could make a huge difference. Sometimes water from a hose was run into the blower to add moisture to the chopped corn if it was too dry at the time of harvest.

A special curved silage fork was used to pull the silage off the wagon. At first it looked like fun, but the girls learned it was actually very hard work. Unloading also could be tricky. If too much silage went into the blower, the pipes would plug. This meant trouble because John would have to be called in from the field to climb up the silo and get the pipes unplugged. That clearly was not his favorite job.

John supervises work on one of the silos, 1984.

It was a good feeling when the Hondls had both silos filled and they could take down the pipes until the next fall. Once in the silo, the corn fermented and by winter, was ready to be fed as silage to the cattle.

The rest of the corn was harvested with a corn picker that picked the entire ear of corn with the kernels still on it. The corn needed to be much drier so it wouldn't spoil and get moldy from too much moisture. Corn could be harvested far into the fall as long as there was no snow in the fields. Again, the Hondls had to hire someone to open the fields because their corn picker was pulled first by a tractor. Dorothy remembered disliking one job in particular, which was to drive a team of horses to pull a wagon box alongside the corn picker to catch the ears of corn. It was difficult to keep the wagon at the same pace as the picker because the horses sometimes wanted to stop or went too fast. Later, a hitch was used to attach a wagon to the side of the picker eliminating the need for driving alongside.

After the corn was picked, it had to be stored in cribs. In the 1940s, the corn was put in small cribs made of snow fence. Then, in 1952, a large new corncrib was built east of the barn. An elevator was set up to transfer the golden ears of corn up to the roof opening and down into the crib. Each wagonload had to be shoveled off by hand into the elevator. The girls built some arm muscle from that task, but Uncle Clement did the majority of the unloading. Nadine can still recall the steady hum and clank of the elevator flights running while she shoveled the ear corn to empty a wagon. When the elevator stopped, the quiet was very satisfying. Later on, grain wagons with a false front similar to that of the silage wagons made unloading less demanding.

Nadine and Bernadette help John get ear corn from a snow fence crib, late 1940s.

It took many days to fill the big crib. The full ears of corn were stored there to dry. Most of the ears were shelled for grinding. The Hondls hired someone with a corn sheller to take the kernels off the ears. Eventually, farm machinery technology progressed and combines came with a corn head attachment that would pick and shell the corn for selling or storing in bins on the farm.

Not all of the ear corn, however, was shelled for grinding. Some of it was fed directly to the pigs, a chore that was not a favorite for the girls. John would drive a wagonload of ear corn into the pig yard and leave it there. At feeding time, the girls would climb quietly over the fence and try to reach the wagon before the hungry pigs realized they were there. But the pigs knew the routine and the girls had to run fast so they would not be surrounded by the hungry animals. As they threw the ears of corn out of the wagon, the girls counted out seventy-five ears or whatever amount John specified. As an animal-lover, Colleen worried that the ears of corn dropping on the pigs' backs would hurt them. But the pigs were tough; nothing fazed them when they wanted to eat.

Cropland surrounds the Hondl farm site, viewed from the south, in the early 1970s. Evergreen windbreak is well established; feedlot and cattle shed for beef operation are in use.

Soybeans Join the Crop Lineup

In reports from the Southeastern Minnesota Farm Management Services, soybeans were first mentioned as a crop in 1939,[18] but it wasn't until the late 1950s that it became more commonplace to plant them. The Hondls started raising soybeans at about this time. The crop could be a good moneymaker and contribute to crop diversity. There was definitely a market since farmers had initially started using soy protein imported from China to improve their livestock feed. The soybeans were harvested with the Massey-Harris 27 combine using a special bean head attachment. Across Minnesota, farmers practiced crop rotation alternating corn and soybeans on their fields year by year.

Grinding Feed for the Livestock

Grinding feed for the animals was a weekly chore and a special challenge in the winter months. Since the oats were already stored in the granary, the feed grinding took place there. A stationary grinder was accessible from the granary door. The large McCormick-Deering tractor was positioned about thirty feet from the granary and a long wide belt placed on the tractor pulley connected it to the feed grinder pulley. Oats were shoveled down from the top bins with shelled corn brought in from the corncrib. Depending on which animals the feed was being made for, a "concentrate" mixture was added that contained minerals, vitamins and other feed stuffs. The proportions were mentally computed by noting the bushels of corn put in by the number of shovel scoops, perhaps not as scientific a method as nowadays when animal nutrition consultants are hired and every part of the feed ration is precisely weighed out.

11

A Bit of the West Under a Minnesota Sky

Whether it was intended or just gradually happened, John had transformed a portion of his Minnesota farm into a kind of western style ranch. His beef herd was small by western standards but John found satisfaction in managing the seventy-five cows and their calves that grazed on the plentiful pasture in the summer. His land produced abundant hay and silage for feed in the winter. Wheat, a mainstay crop in the West, was not often grown in Steele County, but John tried it and successfully harvested many golden fields of wheat as a cash crop. It seemed that John's Big Sky dreams, which began with stories and visits to and from his Uncle Paul in Montana, were fulfilled under the Minnesota sky. John, with Dorothy at his side, had clearly put his own brand on the Hondl land legacy.

Just as his ancestors from Europe had taken huge risks when they journeyed here to secure fertile land, John used his instincts and hard work to make major changes to his crop and livestock mix. By borrowing ideas from western cattle raisers and continually adopting new technology, he found a way to ensure that the Hondl land would continue to support his family far into the future.

As beef cattle graze in the pasture, the Hondl farm has a western look, summer 1985. Wheat fields, oak woods and farm buildings make a tranquil scene.

Part Two: 'Who needs boys, he's got us' - The Daughters Tell Their Stories

All three Hondl girls became pretty adept at most of the farm tasks their dad had them do; if they did not get it right at first, they eventually learned. Nadine recalled when someone said to her, "It's too bad your Dad didn't have boys." She responded, "Who needs boys, he's got us."

As we share our stories we will use the first person to capture more intimately our impressions and memories of family life on the farm in the 1940s, 50s, 60s and 70s. Looking back, we now realize just how close our family became as we worked together to plant and harvest and how each family member, even as a youngster, could contribute to the family's well-being – for example, the haymaking and fence-making definitely come to mind. The lessons learned growing up as farm daughters have served us well in our adult lives. We were given responsibility early and learned to face the consequences of our actions. The high expectations, sometimes reserved for farm boys, were definitely set just as high for the Hondl daughters.

Bernadette, age nine; Colleen, two; Nadine, eleven, July 1953.

Dorothy with her daughters on First Communion day for Nadine and Bernadette, 1953.

12

The Foursquare

We grew up in a big white foursquare farmhouse with dormers, an attic and a dirt-floored basement. The main house was a 1918 addition to the original small two-story, two-bedroom house where Dad and seven brothers and sisters grew up. Because it was an addition to an existing home, the main part of the house was not completely typical of the American Foursquare style popular from the mid-1890s through the later 1930s. But it did have the three attic dormers with a big open space underneath the roof, a wide front porch complete with wooden pillars, four bedrooms on the second floor and archways between the dining room and the living room and also to the stairway. Woodwork and cabinetry, including a beautiful china cupboard and bookshelves with glass doors in the living room, were built in a simple Craftsman style.

In the old part of the house, a stairway led from the washroom to the original two bedrooms. The walls remained the same shade of green that Dad detested even as a child. After the addition was completed, the old back stairway and two bedrooms were used mainly for storage and never repainted.

Likewise, the big attic was unfinished and not used much. However, it did invite the presence of a most unwelcome critter, the bat. At least once a summer, a bat would somehow slip down from the attic and end up in the main part of the house. Someone would be wakened in the middle of the night by the characteristic beating of the bat's wings as it circled inside one of the bedrooms. Pretty soon everyone would be up and Dad would be chasing the bat with a broom. Even though we girls did not believe the old wives' tale of bats getting tangled in one's hair, we still wanted the bat gone.

Winters in the Big House

Since it was not well insulated, the farmhouse was drafty and cold in the winter. Originally, hot water radiators attempted to heat the house, but they were not very successful given the depth of Minnesota winters. We often came downstairs to get dressed because it was too cold in the upstairs bedrooms.

The kitchen was the warmest place, and that's where we spent most of our time December through March. Dad loved the combination wood-burning-and-gas range that baked, cooked and heated water as well as the entire kitchen. He enjoyed sitting with his feet on the oven door, right next to the stove's wood-burning side, which could also be used as a cooking surface in the winter. We burned a variety of fuels, depending on our economic circumstances. When times were tight, we burned corncobs, which attracted mice in the basement and throughout the house. Wood and coal also fueled the stove some winters. Right from his sitting position, Dad could add wood or cobs to the stove to keep everyone cozy.

When Nadine and Bernadette were in grade school, a typical winter kitchen scene would include Dad sitting with his feet up on the oven door and Bernadette standing by the reservoir of the stove reading a book. Nadine would be helping Mom with baking or working on a school project. Mom never got to be a teacher, but we think she would have made a good one. She enjoyed creating simple activities to help us learn. For example, we sometimes played a game to see how many words we could make using the letters of a long word or phrase like Merry Christmas or Happy Halloween. We also would try to list rhyming words. There was a kid's page in *The Farmer* magazine that Mom helped us complete. She dictated our spelling words to us and practiced our multiplication tables with us.

By the time Colleen was born, we began spending more wintertime relaxing in the dining room around an oil-burning stove that had replaced the coal-burning furnace in the basement. This stove was even less efficient in heating the huge house. We sat around the heater basically to keep warm. From that spot we read the paper, did homework, mended clothes and ironed. We kept an orange vinyl sofa near the wall by the heater for sitting and Dad's naps. The stove had a fan to circulate the heat but we found it perfect for drying clothes and our hair. A weekly challenge in winter was drying laundry, which we would hang throughout the house since we had no clothes drier. Sometimes we hung long underwear and overalls outside on the clothesline; they would be frozen stiff when we brought them in to finish drying. The upstairs bedrooms were even colder than they had been with the radiator heat system, but somehow we stayed warm under the covers. Eventually, a new furnace was installed and the radiators were repaired. We returned to the original hot water heating system.

Quick Trip to the Outhouse

Before indoor plumbing was installed in 1959, the Hondl family used a two-seater outhouse a few yards behind the old block garage. Hot and smelly in the summer; unflinchingly cold in late fall and winter, the outhouse was a quick stop for all who visited it. Toilet tissue was a luxury sometimes extended by using the thin paper wrappers from crates of peaches or even newspaper. We girls got a bit of a reprieve during the coldest months when a pail was kept in the freezing back stairway off the washroom for our use. The new bathroom and indoor plumbing were probably the improvements we girls appreciated the most.

The foursquare farmhouse with original dormers and porch columns, May 1968.

A new roof and front porch renovations update the farmhouse, July 1968.

The Foursquare Gets a New Look

As with all houses, maintenance and repairs were needed on the big white house. In 1968, the roof required new shingles and, during the process, the three roof dormers were also removed. Thus, one of Colleen's favorite places to look out at the countryside was taken away. In retrospect, taking off the dormers was probably a good move as it helped to save on heat loss through the roof. Energy saving efforts continued many years later to help farm house renters save on their liquid propane bill. The three daughters and son-in-law Don Gengler all worked together to empty everything out of the attic and install more insulation.

The front porch also was redone in 1968 with new pillars, a cement patio-like area and new steps to the front door. In later years, when the grandchildren visited in the summer, the front porch became a great play area. The granddaughters would scavenge for play items and materials. Setting up a pretend house was a popular activity. They also would shell out corn and put wheat into ordinary containers and set up their store.

13

Squeezing Out the Last Dollar

Like many farm families we were land rich but cash poor. We practiced frugality out of necessity but we also accepted it as the norm and did not feel deprived. One area where we definitely economized was grocery purchases. Of course, as a farm family, we had an advantage because we obtained much of our own food through gardening, canning and freezing, plus butchering livestock for fresh pork, beef and chicken. Purchased foods, however, were considered a luxury and we kept portions small to make them go farther. For example, a small package of JELL-O gelatin or pudding intended to serve four was always divided into six portions at our house. A 12-ounce can of Campbell's condensed soup also was extended to give six people each a small serving. For recipes that called for expensive ingredients such as walnuts, dates or chocolate chips, we used just half the amount and still got the flavor. Cocoa, coconut, raisins and flavorings were also reduced if possible in our baking. Little did we realize that we were actually saving calories with portion control.

Despite controlling portions of purchased foods, we ate well using foods that were homegrown and plentiful. Fresh cracked eggs that could not be sold were turned into angel food cakes and homemade noodles. As another cost saving measure, we made our own pancake syrup with Watkins maple flavoring; preparing it ourselves was less expensive than store bought syrup. Chicken, turkey and ham bones were boiled for soup and another meal. Leftovers seldom went to waste. We sometimes churned our own butter by shaking cream in a jar – a good job for kids. The quality and texture was not quite the same as creamery butter but it was still butter. Nadine recalled, however, that she did not like the taste of it and would not eat it. As the eldest daughter, Nadine had stronger opinions and tended to be the first to challenge our parents on some issues; the younger sisters, of course, happily let her test the waters. For example, could we get time off from chores to go to a school event or to go swimming? Let Nadine ask!

Bernadette, age four, holds up a freshly butchered rooster. Photo from the late 1940s shows the original screened porch on the Hondl farmhouse.

Nadine, Bernadette and Colleen plant seeds in the family garden, mid 1950s. Outhouse is at far right.

One special treat we all did enjoy was hand-cranked ice cream. The whole family got involved in making it. Dad crushed the ice and salted it;

Mom made the sweet egg and cream mixture. All of us took turns spinning the freezer handle as fast as we could. When the paddle came out coated with delicious fresh ice cream, we all grabbed spoons to sample it. One year, we invited a cousin to a birthday party for Nadine where we proudly served the homemade ice cream. We felt bad when the girl asked why we could not afford store-bought ice cream. Her family also lived on a farm but was not as thrift-conscious as our family tended to be. Years later, Bernadette continued the Hondl tradition of hand-cranking ice cream when raising her own family.

Earning "Luxuries" with Green Stamps

An effective advertising technique in the 1950s and early 60s involved trading stamps, which were given as rewards for making purchases. Gas stations, drugstores and grocery stores, in particular, dangled the bait of Green Stamps or Gold Bond Stamps as incentives to get and keep loyal shoppers. The goal was to collect as many stamps as possible, paste them into books and then trade them in for tempting gifts ranging from blankets, cooking utensils and sets of knives to small appliances and even larger items of furniture and home accessories.

We girls fell for the gimmick and spent many hours drooling over the Green Stamp catalog and sometimes even visiting the Green Stamp redemption store, which was right next to the Piggly Wiggly store in Owatonna. Nadine and Bernadette did most of the stamp pasting, sometimes using cotton soaked in a little water to moisten the stamps so we did not have to lick them. We would dig in Mom's purse and search pockets and drawers to make sure we found all the stamps. When we got five or six books filled, we were excited and could not wait to "spend" them. Sometimes Mom let us choose the redemption items and we would surprise her with gifts for Mother's Day, her birthday or Christmas. Two "luxury" items purchased with Green Stamps were a cookie press, which we used every Christmas to make delicious spritz cookies, and a black and gold metal bookshelf, which for years held our small collection of books and decorative items. Other items included a French fry cutter, which did not work well, and a kitchen thermometer set that helped to make delicious candy and boiled frosting. Perhaps the most valued redemption prize was a *Betty Crocker Cookbook* with a red-and-white checkerboard cover.

Nadine remembered another favorite product promotion. We saved box tops and coupons from Betty Crocker products to get silverware, mainly spoons. The red spoon logo is still used on many of the Betty Crocker cake and frosting mixes today.

Less Frugal Times

Times were indeed lean in the 1950s. Mom and Dad were working on getting the farm paid off, investing in machinery and building their beef herd. Bernadette recalled discussions about the newspaper subscription being cancelled because it was too costly and not a necessity. Sometimes telephone service was eliminated for a few months until cash came in from selling hogs or grain. For a time, the family had no car, instead using a pickup truck for all their driving needs. Eventually things got better. The farm was paid off, and in 1959 some remodeling was done to the house. The old kitchen cupboards were torn out and replaced by new birch ones almost doubling the cupboard area. A white porcelain sink was installed with a window above it. The old cook stove was replaced with a new gas range. In the dining and living rooms, carpet was laid. Dad always said the house didn't make any money but still... what a nice difference it made.

There were more signs of better times. Dad bought a new tractor and also purchased a riding lawnmower. What a treat that was since we daughters did most of the grass cutting! In 1965, Mom and Dad bought a Chrysler New Yorker for a cost of about $4,000. It was a beautiful pearlescent tan with a pink undertone. Inside, the seats were upholstered in a rich burgundy satin fabric. It replaced the 1957 black-and-white DeSoto that had also been a great car.

More proof of their fortunes turning for the better came later. In 1969, Colleen graduated from high school and planned to attend the University of Minnesota as had Bernadette, who had tuition scholarships and worked part-time to cover expenses. Colleen was awarded an honorary scholarship meaning she received commendation but no dollars because the family income was too high. Who knew! Colleen too worked part-time throughout college to assist with the costs.

14

Country School and Town School

Formal education for Nadine and Bernadette began much like their parents' experience, but a few years later, it would change considerably. Nadine and Bernadette walked to District 58 School, the same one-room school their father John had attended, about a half mile south of the farm. Nadine was one of five girls in her class along with cousin Karen Hondl, Shirley Nelson and twins Rita and Ruth Wencl. Nadine completed sixth grade at District 58. Bernadette, who had just one classmate, Donna Nelson, in her grade, completed the fourth grade there. Nadine and Bernadette recalled playing dodge ball and Annie, Annie Over with their classmates. They also enjoyed Christmas programs where every student performed and Santa Claus delivered small gifts.

Our school lunches were much better than what Dad remembered taking to school. However, one time Mom had not had time to shop for groceries and there was nothing suitable to put in our lunches. Bernadette recalled her mother arrived at school just before noon with a wonderful lunch of hot dogs in a Thermos, plus fresh buns and bananas. "We were the envy of our classmates that day," Bernadette said.

After six years at District 58 School, Mom and Dad decided it was time for Nadine and Bernadette to attend St. Mary's Catholic School in Owatonna. Bernadette had been getting sick at school and our parents thought maybe the water was not safe or the drinking fountain was not clean. Also, they felt that the education that could be provided in a one-room setting was limited. The first year, 1954, Mom drove us to St. Mary's in Owatonna because the state did not provide bus transportation for parochial students. The following year the rules changed, and we were able to ride the bus. The rules must have changed again; Colleen recalled that the bus company charged ninety dollars per year for parochial students to ride the bus during the time she attended St. Mary's.

To making riding the bus possible for their students, St. Mary's ended the school day a little earlier than Owatonna High School. This allowed elementary students to walk the three blocks to catch the bus at the high school. For Colleen, there was enough extra time to stop in at the little store across from St. Mary's to get a treat or to visit St. Joseph Catholic Church on the way. Since our family did not attend that parish, Colleen thought it was a novelty to stop in and look at all the different statues. It was a beautiful church built in a much different style than Sacred Heart Catholic Church.

Becoming students at St. Mary's meant that tuition had to be paid. Nadine and Bernadette both worked at small jobs, including helping in the school kitchen, to offset some of the tuition costs. Both of the girls remembered becoming friends with the cook Libby Pirkl and they were among the few students who liked and ate her barbecued lima beans. Bernadette also scrubbed sinks in the girls' bathrooms but disliked feeling like a "poor farm girl" in front of her city classmates. Bernadette did not recall if other students had similar jobs. As a new fifth grader coming into an established class she did not appreciate anything that made her seem different from the other students. The adolescent urge to fit in prevailed. Of course, we did not realize it then, but we were learning the value of working for our education. We believe our parents' decision to send us to St. Mary's made a huge difference in our lives, encouraging us to pursue higher goals and be better prepared for high school.

Nadine attended St. Mary's for two years, Bernadette for four and Colleen for all six years of grade school. None of the three girls attended kindergarten. Then it was on to the Owatonna Public Schools for all of them. Part of the decision to transfer might have been the tuition cost. In addition, many students from St. Mary's simply chose the public school for more choices in curriculum, sports and other activities. Out of Colleen's St. Mary's class, about a fourth of the students eventually transferred to the public school.

District 58 School eventually closed. In 1967, the Minnesota Legislature determined that a school district should have both an elementary and a secondary program. Districts that did not operate a secondary school, i.e. the one room schoolhouses still scattered throughout Steele and other Minnesota counties, were given until 1971 to merge with a district that provided K-12 education. [19] District 58 chose not to close until the mandated deadline.

15

Putting It on the Table Fast

Our family meals were breakfast, noon dinner, lunch and supper. During the busy times of spring planting, haying and grain and corn harvests, cooking was a challenge for Mom because she was often out in the field herself, sometimes cultivating, side-raking or going to town for parts, baler twine or whatever was needed. Thus, meals needed to be prepared ahead as much as possible or needed to include something that we girls could put together ourselves. A strategy that we learned was to have the table set before Dad got in the house. To him that meant the meal could not be far behind. He might rest on the couch or read the paper for a few minutes and by then Mom would be in the house to help us put the finishing touches on a meal.

What we ate for each meal also fell into a pattern. We often peeled potatoes around 10:00 A.M. and kept them in cold water until it was time to boil them. We picked and cleaned lettuce, green beans and peas right after breakfast, so they would be ready for cooking. Hearty oven-roasted meats, pan-fried hamburgers and hamburger-noodle goulash kept us going at the noon meal. For suppers, we relied on leftovers to make hash, macaroni and cheese, deviled eggs, potato salad or tuna casserole.

Family Favorites

Angel food cake became a frequent treat as we looked for recipes that used the many broken eggs that could not be sold. Mom perfected this recipe over the years and came to prefer using powdered sugar rather than granulated. She excelled at it long after we discontinued raising chickens and selling eggs. In fact, in 2007 Mom won the grand champion ribbon for baked goods at the Steele County Fair for her angel food cake.

Nadine, with Colleen and Bernadette in 1961, celebrates her eighteenth birthday with an angel food cake.

Dorothy wins the grand champion ribbon for baked goods at the 2007 Steele County Fair for her angel food cake.

Another family treat was spring chicken. If the fryers got big enough by July Fourth, we enjoyed fresh fried chicken for the holiday and for many Sunday dinners following in the summer. "When I say fresh, I mean the chicken was butchered and served within a few hours and tasted amazingly better than most chicken one buys today," Bernadette recalled. One other favorite was Murphy dish, which combined scalloped potatoes with ham, carrots and onion. It was an inexpensive yet basic casserole recipe courtesy of a salesman for Murphy Livestock Feeds.

Our garden produced most of our summer vegetable dishes. Among the favorites were spring leaf lettuce with bacon or doused with vinegar and cream, sweet corn and green peppers, garden peas in milk, yellow beans with a white sauce sharpened with vinegar, beef vegetable soup simmered with beets and carrot tops and cucumbers in cream served over mashed potatoes. Dad loved Mom's baked beans, which started with soaking the beans overnight and then slow baking them with a ham hock. We ate cherry cobbler, apple crisp and most any kind of quick dessert with fruit in summer and fall. Mom excelled at pies, especially peach, apple and blueberry. We also enjoyed lemon snow, lemon cake pudding, sherbet and pineapple upside down cake with some of the recipes coming from the *Betty Crocker Cookbook*.

Dietary Dilemma

An extra challenge for meal planning was to prepare something special for Dad when he was having an ulcer flare up. After being diagnosed with bleeding ulcers, Dad chose not to go with the first line of treatment to have a portion of his stomach removed. The doctor then recommended a mild, low-fiber diet with more milk and dairy products, which was standard treatment at that time. As alternatives for Dad we frequently made mashed potatoes, tapioca pudding, Cream of Wheat, scrambled eggs or cooked fruit. He ate boiled ham instead of baloney in sandwiches and avoided spicy foods. Reducing stress also was encouraged but Dad found that hard to do, especially during the intense work seasons spring through fall. He typically lost fifteen pounds over the summer and fall seasons and regained it over the winter months.

In spite of his digestive problems, Dad liked to try different foods, including various kinds of cheese from the Cheese Caves in Faribault, Minnesota, pickled herring, oysters and special kinds of smoked fish and sausage. One of his unusual requests was for lutefisk, a Norwegian delicacy, very popular and served prior to Christmas at many local Lutheran church suppers. Nadine brought it home for us to sample. The fish has a jelly-like consistency with not much flavor and Dad was not a fan after all. The buttered lefse sprinkled with sugar, which we also tried, was much tastier.

Dorothy at ninety-four, still enjoys making kolaches (poppy seed biscuits), 2014.

Kolaches, a Czech Favorite

One baked delicacy was based on our Czech roots. We enjoyed making and eating kolaches, which are yeast rolls with a fruit filling. Mom would make the dough and then pat out a small amount into a rough square placing a prune or poppy seed filling on the square. Next, she would take the two opposite corners, pinch them together in the middle and do the same with the other two corners. Then she added a streusel topping before baking. Kolaches were delicious throughout the year but a "must have" at Christmas time. In Colleen's travels, she tasted peach kolaches in Prague but noted they were round and open faced. This may be the original way kolaches were made. Dozens of kolaches are still sold at the annual summer festival at Holy Trinity Church, Litomysl. They are also sold in four different bakeries and grocery stores at New Prague, a Minnesota town with Czech heritage, as well as other towns where Czech immigrants settled.

China and Linen for the Holidays

Holiday meals took on celebration status and were served in the dining room using Mom's good china, silverware, linen tablecloth, napkins and a centerpiece. Food was the focus, and Dad would get involved with helping to choose which kind of meat would be served. Thanksgiving options might have been duck, goose or turkey. Christmas choices were ham or turkey, depending on what we had served on Thanksgiving. Easter generally called for ham or lamb. As we girls got older, we loved helping Mom expand the menus to include fancy desserts and new salads from the *Betty Crocker Cookbook*. We also made many Christmas sweet treats: divinity fudge with walnuts, English almond toffee, coffee cookies, lemon tea bread, spritz and cut-out sugar cookies. On Easter Mom's roast lamb with lemon sauce was always a crowd pleaser, as was a layered pineapple and lemon JELL-O salad served on lettuce leaves.

One Thanksgiving dinner that was not so successful occurred when Nadine was about eight years old and Bernadette was seven. It had been a wet, late fall harvest; Dad and Mom were out picking corn on that holiday. We girls were supposed to keep an eye on the duck roasting in the oven. By the time Mom arrived in the house, the duck was burned to a crisp. We felt bad and Dad was pretty disappointed too since he was used to Mom's good holiday meals. Mom, no doubt, saved the day with enough side dishes prepared earlier so no one went hungry. For years, Dad had some fun teasing us about the "burned-duck Thanksgiving."

Winter holidays gave us more time to celebrate at the table, but even during the regular work season we bonded around the kitchen table, appreciating food and enjoying each other's company. When field work was underway, it was a challenge to get all six of us, including Uncle Clement, at the table at one time, but we tried because it didn't feel right when someone had to eat alone. At noon, we served a full meal, with bread and butter always on the table. Usually we had dessert too. The family usually took at least an hour break to eat and relax before heading out to a long afternoon of tractor driving or making hay. Mealtimes were lively, sometimes involving conversation about politics or what was going on in the neighborhood. But most often the discussions focused on the farm operation: which bills needed to be paid, who to hire to help with baling, when to start cutting the wheat, what jobs needed doing that afternoon, were we going to make hay or go for a picnic on Sunday. As our parents talked about farming decisions big and small, we daughters felt included and knew that we too could do things to help out.

16

Sunday Drives

Entertainment was definitely a low-budget item in our family and also unplanned, due to the fact that Dad's philosophy was that one should not relax unless one's work was completed. We all know that a farmer's work is never done, thus entertaining activities or outings only occurred at the rare times when it was too wet, too hot or otherwise impossible to work.

Sunday drives were a favorite activity because they met all the criteria: cheap, spontaneous and possible to accomplish in a couple of hours. Before we went on a drive, usually after dinner on Sunday, Dad would shave and put on some Sportsman aftershave lotion; it smelled like Sunday. We filled up the car at the gas barrel where we usually fueled the tractors. Mom would drive. Dad would be in the copilot seat and the three daughters sat in the back. The first decision came at the end of the driveway. Should we go north or south? If we went south, we might head to St. Olaf Lake to watch other people boat or fish, to Blooming Prairie or on a long drive to Austin to visit the Authfather family. If we went north, we might end up in Waseca, Shieldsville, Faribault or other spots, usually around a lake or something scenic.

Along the way, Dad gave us a running commentary about who owned various farms, when the barn burned down, who married whom and what breed of cattle or hogs they liked to raise. Usually we found a small store, root beer stand or Dairy Queen along the way for a treat. Sometimes Mom remembered she needed a few groceries and we would pick them up if we were near one of the small stores in Steele Center, Pratt or Blooming Prairie.

One of our favorite Sunday driving activities was looking at houses in Owatonna. We would take the Austin Road into town and drive past the new "ramblers" being built in the southeast section of Owatonna. Mom and Dad always thought $10,000 would buy one of those houses, and for years they toyed with the idea of quitting farming and buying a house in town. It was mostly a pipe dream that looked appealing when they felt tired from all the hard work of farming and was never seriously pursued. Dad actually loved his farmland very much and was proud of the place he was continually improving. He used to come home from trips out West and say, "Minnesota farm land still looks the best."

Even more treasured than the house hunting excursions in Owatonna was going to Mineral Springs Park, the family's favorite destination. Dad and Mom often stayed in the car and watched people picnicking, playing ball or playing horseshoes while we girls enjoyed the swings, slides and merry-go-round. Sometimes we would bring a picnic and grill hamburgers or hot dogs. The big attraction for Dad was the spring water. He enjoyed getting a cool drink and marveling at how the water flowed continuously from the ground. The other big draw for us was the Dairy Queen on the way to Mineral Springs Park and Dartts Park. Our family consumed dozens of five or ten-cent soft ice cream cones over the years. Sometimes Dad splurged and ordered a thirty-five cent hamburger or a fifty-cent shake. For about a dollar, if you didn't count gas, we had a wonderful family Sunday afternoon. The ride home always took too long for us girls and, inevitably, by the time we passed Jerome Hartle's farm, less than a mile from home, we were fighting and whining in the back seat. Dad and Mom knew the ride had been long enough.

The Sunday drives would continue years later when Mom and Dad visited Colleen and her family on their farm at Iona, Minnesota. This time, it would be Dad and Don taking a drive, often to the Chandler area. That was one of Dad's favorite routes as the area reminded him of being out West.

Another special destination in later years was Nadine's country home near Rogers, Minnesota. Mom and Dad would drive there to visit and enjoy gourmet Sunday dinners prepared by Nadine and her significant other Tom Workman, who loved to cook and entertain. Tom often served some of the fresh fish he had caught or wild game he had hunted. When Mom and Dad spent the night, they were served a big breakfast the next morning, typically fresh sausage and biscuits, Tom's specialty.

17

Prince, Prince, Rex, Tiger and Snappy

We'd be remiss if we did not talk about the family pets. First, there were the dogs beginning with a mutt called Buster followed by two dogs named Prince. When Prince I died, we immediately got another white German Shepherd just like him. Colleen loved trying to stage pictures of Prince II. Her goal was to get action shots for a 4-H photography project. She took pictures of him jumping over the gate of the cattle shed and leaping for a dog treat, but her favorite was of him in the old Dodge pickup. It wasn't exactly an action shot, but the picture shows how happy Prince II was to be going for a ride. It was a sad day when he died of unknown causes. Colleen recalled going with Dad to bury him. Even Dad had tears in his eyes as we said goodbye to him.

Prince II loved his rides in the old Dodge pickup, 1969.

After all of the girls were out of the house, someone gave Mom and Dad a dog named Rex. He was a large collie with the annoying habit of barking furiously and jumping up and down whenever the old Oliver diesel tractor was started up. Who knows why he would do that, but it happened every time. Rex was a nice dog as were later additions Hercules and Pepper, two dogs that Mom and Dad got after Rex, but none of them came close to having proud personalities like the two Princes.

Dogs weren't the only pets on the farm. Every farm had to have cats, too. Over the years, there were many favorite cats. Two that come to mind are Tiger and Snappy, cats given to the Hondls by Colleen's friend Theresa Nass. After Theresa's cat had a large litter, the Nass family needed to find homes for them. Two other cats, with names long forgotten, were a mother-daughter pair of identically marked black-and-white cats.

Although pets were important on the farm, they typically remained outside, which was standard practice on farms. One did not pamper farm cats or dogs other than providing good shelters for them. However, Colleen would occasionally "invite" a cat into the house. One time, when Colleen invited in the black-and-white mother cat, she forgot about the cat in the house. It wandered into the upstairs storeroom and somehow the door got shut leaving the cat inside. A couple of days later, the family heard meowing. The cat had made herself a nest and had a litter of kittens! Surprisingly Mom and Dad weren't too upset about the mess, but the cat and her kittens were quickly moved outside. Maybe there was a little lenience in the situation with Colleen being the youngest. As they say, the youngest in the family always has it the easiest.

Populations of farm cats rise and fall. During a down time in the late 1980s, Dad decided he needed more cats to keep the mice under control in the barn. So, Colleen and Don brought over several cats from their farm's abundant supply. The cats weren't too happy being transported that far, but they and their offspring were around for a long time.

Cats remained on the farm long after Mom moved to Owatonna. For many years, she purchased cat food for them and the house renters fed them in the barn. However, these cats were no longer friendly pets with no one around to pay attention to them.

18

Summer Vacations and Who Was Left Behind

As we three girls got a little older, Mom and Dad began taking summer trips out West. These were not necessarily vacations for the entire family as the girls sometimes stayed home with Uncle Clement to do chores and take care of the farm. The trips usually occurred after the oats harvest had been completed and before fall harvest began. Not only did Mom and Dad visit Uncle Paul in Circle, Montana, but they also explored the ranches where some of their cattle originated. They also enjoyed going to Yellowstone National Park several times and Glacier National Park at least once. On one trip to Yellowstone with another couple, the black bears got very friendly. There was a scratch on the 1957 black-and-white DeSoto passenger side door to prove it. Dad also told us about the bears tipping over the garbage cans at night as they looked for an easy meal.

A bear leaves his mark on the DeSoto during the Hondl's trip to Yellowstone National Park in the late 1950s.

In the summer of 1962, Bernadette and Uncle Clement had farm duty when Mom, Dad, Nadine and Colleen went on a vacation to the Black

Hills, Mount Rushmore and Yellowstone National Park. Bernadette was chosen to stay home because Colleen was too young and Nadine, already working as a hairdresser in Austin, Minnesota, considered this her summer vacation. One job Bernadette remembered was shoveling the ground feed into gunnysacks for her uncle. He then carried each bag, weighing ninety to one hundred pounds, on his shoulder from the granary to the pigs and cattle in their various locations. Bernadette had to make sure all the livestock were watered and, if any pigs or cattle got out, she and Uncle Clement would have to get them back to their pens. Bernadette also prepared and served all their meals.

In the late 1960s, Mom and Dad went on another vacation leaving Colleen home with some expectant sows. She was instructed to give iron shots to the newly born little pigs and clip their teeth. This was not an easy job for anyone as the wiggly, squirming little pigs were hard to hang onto. The teeth clipping was necessary for the comfort of the sow when the pigs nursed. When Mom and Dad got home there was some needed "repair" work on the teeth-clipping job.

In a diary Bernadette kept during 1959-60, she expressed some resentment on the part of the teenage girls when they were left home during their parents' trips. She wrote: "Mom and Dad are gone again." "I bet they won't buy any cattle this time either." "Just when we wanted to do something with our friends in Owatonna, Mom and Dad decided to go to South Dakota." Now we realize that our parents had trusted us with taking care of one of their most prized possessions and their livelihood – the farm and all the livestock. They were teaching responsibility and we were learning it.

Whoever stayed home was excited for the family's return and to see what souvenirs they acquired. One that stands out for Bernadette was a miniature log cabin that burned pine incense. "To this day whenever I am out in nature and smell pine woods I think of that little log cabin," she recalled. Colleen especially enjoyed a package of seashells and the rock samples including a piece of petrified wood. Nadine loved taking photos of flowers and collecting postcards with pictures of scenic views and native plants.

19

Our 4-H Club, the Pratt Commandoes

When Nadine and Bernadette were eleven and nine years old, Mom and Dad took them to join the Pratt Commandoes 4-H Club. When asked how the decision to join 4-H came about, Mom said she and Dad thought "it would be good for you girls to be in 4-H and learn new skills with other young people nearby." The club was made up of the neighborhood families including the Warner, Granowski, Schuster, Ptacek, Henry, Grubisch, Christofferson and Neigebauer families. Later on, we were joined by the Wrede, Oeltjenbruns, Hartle and Homuth families. We met regularly at the old town hall in Pratt. In later years, we had club meetings at the large white 4-H building on the Steele County fairgrounds.

Summer Tours and "Home Ec" Checkups

In the summer, the 4-H club tour was a big event. All the families drove around to each member's farm place to see their livestock and gardening projects. The county agent or the 4-H club agent came along and offered a critique and tips on the progress of the projects. At noon, there was a wonderful potluck picnic at one member's farm place. Although we never hosted the picnic, we spent a lot of time getting the yard and garden perfect for the tour. Years later, Colleen began working for the University of Minnesota Extension Service, a major outreach institution of the University. Larry Tande, our former 4-H club agent who was then in a different role with Extension, reminisced with Colleen about how beautiful the Hondl farm place was when he visited on those tours.

We also had "Home Ec" checkups in the summer. The home demonstration agent came out to the event for each club. Members were to bring a sample of their food, clothing or home improvement projects. Then the agent would comment and offer suggestions for improvement similar to what was done on the tours. In about 1967, Mom and Colleen volunteered to host the checkup. We spent a lot of time cleaning and getting ready for the big day. We all sat around the dining room with our projects on the table. Joann Ross was the agent who came. Later on, Colleen's first Extension job was in Cottonwood County, where Joann Ross Nickel lived after having left Steele County.

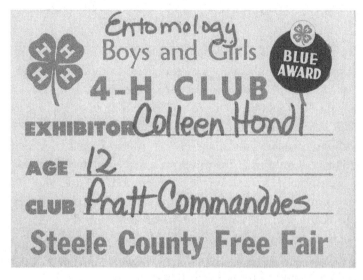

Colleen serves as president of the Pratt Commandoes 4-H Club in 1967.

Hands-on Learning with Projects

Nadine and Bernadette typically took on several 4-H projects, including vegetable gardening, bread baking, clothing construction and showing pigs. One major activity was the silent bread-baking contest where one mixed and shaped a loaf of white bread while under the scrutiny of a judge. There were also oral demonstrations. One year, Nadine and Bernadette won a state fair trip for their team oral bread demonstration, which involved measuring the ingredients, mixing the dough and shaping a loaf of white bread. It was a big deal to take the bus to the Minnesota State Fair in St. Paul, stay overnight in the 4-H dormitory and eat breakfast with kids from all over the state. Bernadette and Nadine still remember looking out to the state fair crowd as they gave their demonstration and seeing their mom, dad and Colleen in the audience.

As 4-H continued on, more projects were added, including photography and entomology. Colleen took the basics but never did try the bread project. She enjoyed entomology and, while picking sow thistles or mustard plants for Dad, she would bring along a collecting jar to capture insects for her fair display. She also won a state fair trip with photography one year. The next year, Colleen talked Mom into setting up a darkroom in the bathroom to make contact prints from negatives. The chemicals and paper were purchased at a camera store in Faribault. The bathroom had to be completely dark so a blanket was placed over the window and towels stuffed by the door jam. Since it was summer and the window could not be opened, it got pretty hot in there. However, the judge at the fair did not seem to appreciate the extra effort – there was no state fair trip that year.

Eyes on the Prize - the County Fair

The county fair was the highlight of our summers. All of us girls spent many days getting our projects ready for the fair. Steele County had a big 4-H program with perhaps 700 members during the time we were in 4-H. With such a large membership, we were allowed to bring only one item per project to the fair.

The most lucrative project was showing and selling our pigs at the fair. During the year, we fed and cared for our market barrows together in the west pen in the barn. We would take them out in the yard to "train" them with a yardstick to get them to walk, not run, in the fair show ring.

Getting our Poland China barrows, one breed of pigs we raised, to the fair, however, could be a challenge. We did not have a pickup at that time, so had to use the big red Dodge livestock truck to haul them. Once at the fair, pigs were judged by breed, and we always did very well with our pigs in our class, usually earning blue ribbons.

One year, we had really nice pigs with good contours and full hams. The county agent on the tour advised us that one could be a trip winner. The other also had good conformation but would be a little too big by fair time. The better pig was Colleen's, but she was too young to be eligible to go to the State Junior Livestock Show in September. Years later, she expressed some regret about insisting on taking the smaller pig to the fair, "I should have let Bernadette take the pig to the fair as it could have won a trip to the Junior Livestock Show."

On Saturday of the fair, the 4-H Livestock Auction was held. Local businesses "purchased" the animals, paying a premium on top

Colleen leaves the 4-H show ring with a blue ribbon for her Spotted Poland China barrow at the Steele County Fair in 1966.

of the market price. Dad was always very interested to see which business purchased our pigs as it could be influenced by how much he had bought from businesses during the year. Bernadette once received fifty-eight cents a pound for her barrow, the top price paid that year. In later years, fair officials limited how much of a premium price could be paid to make the auction more equitable for the young sellers. Although it was nice to get the check, it was hard to say goodbye to the pigs as they had become pets by that time.

We also got involved in other aspects of the county fair. We entered items from past 4-H clothing projects in open class. Sometimes we took food items, too. It was a good way to earn extra premium money. Colleen also enjoyed going to the U.S. Department of Agriculture display and

90

picking up free publications. It was a first glimmer of the possibilities for Extension work beyond 4-H.

20

Entertainment Home Style

Let's Stop at the Library

Books were practically nonexistent in our home, so we depended heavily on the Owatonna Public Library for our reading materials. If Mom had a few extra minutes during her frequent trips to Owatonna for machinery parts and groceries, we girls would always try to include a stop at the library.

Colleen liked picking out her own books, but she didn't always get to. Often Mom would bring home a stack. That was fun, too, as it was a surprise. Bernadette and Nadine also remember selecting books for Colleen. She was the most avid reader and sometimes disappeared for hours sitting up in a tree or even on the chicken house roof to read. Her older sisters got a little annoyed when she avoided her chores with a book. All of us girls remembered reading a lot of biographies, the orange-covered short and sanitized series appropriate for children. Colleen recalled that many of them were about baseball players. Bernadette remembered reading plays one summer, including Shakespeare. She also recalled how grown up she felt when she was able to check out books from the adult section on the main floor of the library.

Colleen joined the library summer reading program for several years. She remembered receiving a little book in which to write the title, author and a few sentences about each book she read. It was good practice for writing skills! There was a party on the top floor of the library at the end of the program. Colleen won a book one year.

Reading was also a family activity, especially in the winter. Since Dad's limited education prevented him for doing a lot of reading on his own, he liked to listen to stories or magazine articles that Mom and we girls would take turns reading aloud. The James Herriot books and westerns were favorites. We also brought home library books with lots of photos; travel, animals, Native Americans and Western history were favorite subjects. Mom loved to read but did not have much time to do so while we were growing up. After moving to Owatonna, however, she enjoyed reading as much as she liked.

Not only was the Owatonna Public Library our chief source of books as we grew up, it became a convenient and safe meeting spot for our family. In junior high and high school, if we had an activity after school and Mom could not get there until later, the library would be our designated pick-up spot. Built in 1899 at the corner of Elm and Broadway, the beautiful Classical Revival library building is now on the National Register of Historic Places. We spent many an afternoon waiting on those elegant steps for a ride home. When we girls were old enough to drive, the library continued to be a frequent and favorite destination.

Owatonna Public Library, circa 1940s-50s. Courtesy Owatonna Public Library.

Turn on the Radio

Earlier in our story we mentioned the radio—that little yellow plastic box with the two dials that sat on the kitchen cupboard right next to Dad's chair. It was a regular part of our noon meal as we listened to the stock and grain markets. Throughout the 1950s and early 60s, however, that small communication device also served as our main source of family entertainment. It gave us a variety of music, some good laughs and a link to the outside world.

Bernadette's earliest listening memories started in the late 1940s, probably before she entered first grade. KDHL – 920 AM from Faribault, Minnesota, aired the *Five O'clock Story Hour*, filled with children's recorded stories and music. The station regularly played "Peter and the Wolf," a children's symphony by Prokofiev in which each instrument portrays a different animal. "That made the biggest impression," Bernadette recalled. "It was probably my first experience with classical music and was so different from the polkas and old-time music our parents listened to."

On Saturday and Sunday evenings the whole family would gather around the radio for some of Dad's western favorites including *The Lone Ranger* and *Gunsmoke*. For comedy we all loved Jack Benny, Arthur Godfrey and the *Our Miss Brooks Show*. *Our Gal Sunday*, an afternoon soap opera we girls sometimes listened to, asked the question: "Can this girl from the little mining town in the West find happiness as the wife of a wealthy and titled Englishman?" Of course, we had to find out.

A fun mid-day variety and talk show was *Art Linkletter's House Party*, which originated from Los Angeles. Bernadette remembered learning a bit of California geography from that program. Art would always ask his guests where they were from; most would name some city in California and Art seemed to know just where it was, near San Francisco, close to LA, etc. "I used to try to picture the state of California or even look up in the atlas to see where the towns were located. At the time, those cities seemed like another planet away from our farm in Minnesota," Bernadette remembered.

Although Dad was not interested in sports and considered them a waste of time, some of the girls did become sports fans. Colleen followed the Minnesota Twins baseball team and even knew the starting lineups, thanks to the games broadcast on WCCO radio. Bernadette liked listening to the Minnesota Gopher football games on WCCO when she, as a University of Minnesota student, came home on fall break to help with the corn and soybean harvests. In between driving to and from the fields to pick up wagonloads of grain, Bernadette would run into the house to catch the score and listen to a few plays. Today's farmers have it much easier; they can simply turn on the radios or TV sets in the cab of their tractor or combine to get their news and sports.

Colleen also enjoyed a popular quiz show on WCCO called *Honest To Goodness*. The cohosts Dick Chapman and Randy Merriman would call listeners and ask them a trivia question. If they missed the answer, the jackpot rose by $8.30 (WCCO was 830 on the AM dial). Unfortunately the Hondls did not get to participate because they sometimes did not have phone service, but they still had fun trying to answer the questions.

Rabbit Ears Finally Arrive

Our family did not own a television until 1965. By then, 92.6% of American households had a television.[20] Televisions were expensive at that time and not on Dad's priority list. Nor did we own a record player. Clearly, the Hondl family was a late adopter of entertainment technology. Nadine rectified the television situation for herself, and for the rest of the family to some extent, when she began her first job as a hairdresser. She purchased a portable black-and-white television with her early savings. When Nadine came home for the weekend from her job in Austin, she would sometimes bring her television along. Dad enjoyed that as *Bonanza* on Sunday night was a favorite. Perhaps the Chinese cook Hop Sing on *Bonanza* reminded Dad of his own father's California experience with a Chinese cook! Dad and Colleen would both be disappointed if the back seat of Nadine's car was empty.

When we finally got our own television some of the favorite shows included *I Love Lucy* and *Little House on the Prairie*. Having a television also made some of life's more boring tasks more enjoyable. For Colleen, the television made cleaning eggs more tolerable. "I would get home from school, set up the egg cleaning equipment in the kitchen and then wheel in the television cart from the dining room," she recalled. "Watching television made the boring job go much faster." One of Colleen's favorite shows was *Dark Shadows*, which ran from 1966-71 – a forerunner of today's craze for vampires and werewolves.

Colleen noted that one of her most memorable television moments occurred before her family got a set. On February 9, 1964, she happened to be staying overnight in Owatonna with her friend Theresa Nass, whose family had a television. Theresa and Colleen joined the millions of young Americans who watched The Beatles' first appearance on the *Ed Sullivan Show*. "It was the talk of our seventh grade class the next morning," Colleen remembered. "We thought everything was so different about them including their longer hair and, of course, the music."

Winter Fun on Blades

Minnesota winters frequently made doing farm chores extremely unpleasant, but we girls did enjoy some fun times playing in the plentiful snow and ice. We built snow forts and dug tunnels in the snow banks. Sleds arrived under the Christmas tree one year for Nadine and Bernadette. We spent many hours pulling each other and finding snow banks big enough to slide down. These sleds were passed on to Colleen and later to the granddaughters.

One year, Mom and Dad tried to interest us in roller-skating, but we preferred the windy, chilly, outdoor sport on ice instead. After renting ice skates a few times, we were excited to receive our own pairs of white lace-up ice skates for Christmas. We spent many Sunday afternoons (nine during the 1959-60 winter, according to Bernadette's diary) skating with friends at Warsinski Rink in Morehouse Park in Owatonna. On a few occasions, we tried to skate on a frozen pond in the oak woods north of the farmhouse, but roots and branches sticking up in the ice took the pleasure out of it. Nadine also recalled flooding an area across the driveway to make our own skating area, but it, too, was less fun than going to Warsinski's.

21

Expanding the Family - Girls, Girls, Girls

By 1973 we daughters had all left the farm for independent lives. (More details follow in a later section.) Nadine was working as a hairdresser in the Twin Cities area but still made frequent visits to Mom and Dad on the farm. Bernadette had moved to Ohio for her career in journalism. She married Kenneth Thomasy in 1971 and two daughters, Sara and Clare, followed in 1979 and 1981 respectively. Colleen had accepted her first position with the University of Minnesota Extension Service in southwest Minnesota. She married Don Gengler from Slayton, Minnesota, in 1978. They gave John and Dorothy two more granddaughters, Kimberly in 1983 and Darielle in 1988. The Gengler girls were only a three-hour drive away from the Hondl grandparents.

Meanwhile, with fewer hands to help them with the farm work, Mom and Dad had decided to look for a qualified family to rent the farm. To enable the renter family to occupy the farmhouse while operating the farm, Mom and Dad purchased a three-bedroom mobile home for themselves and installed it south of the farmhouse. Mom was excited about the mobile home because everything was new and conveniently on one level, with a washer and drier next to the kitchen. The three bedrooms seemed spacious for the two of them. Later, when the extended family arrived on visits, it became lively and cozy and we created some of our best family memories there.

As years went by, the renters took the majority of the field work out of Dad's hands, but he and Mom still looked after some livestock and tended to the upkeep of the buildings and farmland. With fewer responsibilities, however, they had been freed up significantly so that they could travel and spend more time visiting their adult children and grandchildren.

John was thrilled to finally be a grandpa even though the grandkids were three hours and three states away. Dad got along very well with young children, talking to them on their level. He loved showing the grandkids the farm animals, taking them on a tractor or wagon ride, and

97

of course, having them around the table at meals. A favorite photo appeared in *Farm and Ranch Living* magazine.[21] It showed Grandpa John sprinkling icy cold well water on two granddaughters in a tiny wading pool set up on the farm lawn. Our Mom, too, was a happy, loving grandparent, patient and sweet, enjoying the gift of being able to watch four more girls grow up, as she had her own daughters. She taught them to bake cut-out cookies, got them involved in picking vegetables from the garden, making pickles and, of course, reading them hundreds of books.

John and Dorothy spend their first winter in the new mobile home installed on the farm in 1974.

Since Mom and Dad lived in the mobile home, the "big house" had an air of mystery for the four granddaughters. If all four were together, invariably they would ask Grandma if they could play in the big house when renters were not living there. Darielle especially enjoyed going over to the house and exploring. All four cousins loved the glass door bookcases in the living room and the open staircase. Clare and Kim dreamed of redecorating the farmhouse someday.

Grandpa John sprinkles cold well water on granddaughters Sara and Clare Thomasy in 1984. The photo appeared in *Farm & Ranch Living* in 1987.

Usually, however, everyone stayed together in the mobile home. Often, when Kim and Darielle visited, we would all relax in the mobile home's living room. The girls enjoyed playing "restaurant" with Grandpa and whoever else would give them food orders. They would "prepare" the orders at the kitchen counter and deliver them only to collect more orders.

In the cozy confines of the mobile home, the play got quite lively when all the granddaughters visited. They had to be continually warned to watch out for their grandpa's spit can, which was often placed on the floor by the couch. Dad had been chewing Copenhagen tobacco for most of his adult life and we daughters were used to the habit. However, the granddaughters found the spitting and the spit can quite fascinating. Since Grandpa liked Copenhagen so much, they wondered why they couldn't have some. In fact, granddaughter Sara recalled that "Grandpa would be grumpy when he ran out."

The daughters and granddaughters enjoy a lively family gathering in 1989. In back: Colleen and Bernadette. Front row, from left: Kimberly Gengler, Clare and Sara Thomasy, Nadine Hondl and Darielle Gengler. Sweatshirts hand painted by Nadine.

Dad was surrounded by female offspring; three daughters and four granddaughters. The thought must have passed his mind many times about what would happen to the farm; it was not likely that any of his daughters or granddaughters would take over as he and his male ancestors traditionally had done. But nationwide, farming economics were changing as well, so that fewer and fewer sons and grandsons were opting for that choice or could afford to take over a farm. Son-in-law Ken was a career teacher; son-in-law Don was running a dairy operation in partnership with his brothers. It seemed that the comment made years earlier to Nadine, "It's too bad your Dad didn't have boys," was no longer relevant.

Granddaughters, from left, Clare, Kimberly, Darielle and Sara enjoy the hot tub at the bed and breakfast family weekend in 1995. The next chapter has more details on this gathering.

22

Travels and Family Adventures

Dad and Mom often dreamed of spending winters in Arizona, Texas, or somewhere warm to get away from the cold Minnesota weather. With fewer farm responsibilities, they enjoyed several major trips together. Dad finally fulfilled his wish to see California one winter when he and Mom flew to Santa Monica to visit Frank and Vivian Beal, relatives of son-in-law Ken. The Beals were wonderful hosts, taking Mom and Dad to Knott's Berry Farm, the *Lawrence Welk Show*, the Santa Monica Pier and other interesting sites in the Los Angeles area.

On another winter vacation, Nadine helped drive Mom and Dad to Texas. They stopped at the National Cowboy and Western Heritage Museum in Oklahoma City, Oklahoma, visited Dolores and Doug McCarty near San Antonio, Texas, and spent time with Uncle Edward and Aunt Mary Warner at McAllen. Dad was fascinated by the Cowboy Museum and brought back a drawing of a cowboy and his horse that he enjoyed for many years. Another historical site that impressed Dad and Mom was the LBJ Ranch, part of the Lyndon Johnson National Historical Park at Stonewall, Texas.

Probably Mom and Dad's longest vacation was to McAllen, Texas, where they rented a small apartment for a month and spent time with the Warners. During their stay, Mom and Dad ventured into Mexico on a two-day bus trip to Monterey. They visited a glass-blowing factory and enjoying seeing the countryside. Mom appreciated the bus ride and not having to drive. She recalled seeing hundreds of old Volkswagen Beetles traveling on the roads in Mexico.

One year, the dream of a winter in sunny Arizona came with a price when Dad and Mom were stranded in Colorado. On the way back from Arizona, they were delayed by a snowstorm for two days near Denver. They spent time at a motel and counted themselves lucky that they were warm and comfortable while others were trying to survive the nights in cold, snow-covered cars.

John and Dorothy mark their fifieth wedding anniversary in 1991 with a family portrait. Front row from left: Nadine, Kimberly and Darielle Gengler, Dorothy, Clare and Sara Thomasy. Back row: Colleen, Don Gengler, John, Ken Thomasy and Bernadette.

Gathered around the table at a picnic in honor of John and Dorothy's golden anniversary, clockwise from left are: Kimberly, Clare, Darielle, Sara, Nadine, Ken, John, Don, Bernadette and Dorothy. Colleen took the photo, 1991.

The More We Get Together

For a number of summers, the Hondls and their extended families made time to gather together, often at bed and breakfast inns two or three hours from the Hondl farm. The first such outing was in 1994 when we spent a few days at Clear Lake, Iowa, renting a house on the lake shore. We enjoyed the beaches, a lake cruise and celebrated Bernadette's fiftieth birthday. Dad liked to go for one boat ride each summer, so we fulfilled his wish that year at Clear Lake.

Sometimes the gatherings were planned nearer the Genglers' home. They had a harder time getting away since Don was a dairy farmer with daily responsibilities. One year we met to celebrate Mom and Dad's fiftieth wedding anniversary at Round Lake, Minnesota. We took over the Painted Prairie Bed and Breakfast with the four cousins staying together in a little trailer near the main house. Dad enjoyed chatting with the B&B owners who bred and raised Painted Pony horses on their lakefront property. Other gatherings were at Okoboji, Iowa, and Jackson, Minnesota. The summer family tradition provided a fun and relaxing time since no one had to do all the cooking and hosting. Plus, it got Mom and Dad off the farm for a few days. It was "good cousin time" as well.

Anyone Need a Haircut?

When extended family was visiting at the Hondl home, a typical scene would find the kitchen table littered with hair rollers, chemicals, clips and combs, as Nadine set up shop under less than ideal conditions. Nadine has been a professional hair stylist and our family hairdresser for most of her adult life. Whenever possible, Mom and the sisters visited Nadine at her salon in Austin or later in the Minneapolis area, but most often it was more convenient for Nadine to come to us with her skills. Mom, in particular, was grateful for Nadine because Mom readily admitted she could not get the hang of curling and styling her own hair. At a conservative estimate of three permanents and maybe six cuts a year, that adds up to 150 perms and 300 haircuts Nadine has given Mom over the past fifty years. Nor would Dad go elsewhere to get his hair cut, even if it got extra-long. He said he only wanted Nadine to cut it. We felt a little guilty asking Nadine to work on her days off but she was always happy to work at her profession of "making people beautiful."

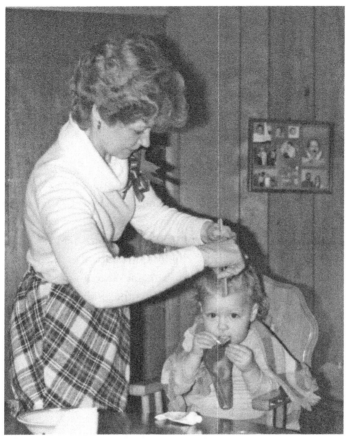

Nadine gives Sara Thomasy, eighteen months old, a haircut in the kitchen of the Hondl mobile home.

With the advances in hair color, Nadine also kept us looking young. Even Dad joined the believers in the benefits of hair color. When his hair started going gray in his early seventies, Nadine gave him some warm brown tones and for years Dad's neighbors and friends were amazed that he looked so young. It was part of Dad's long-time effort to remain fit and young. He always stood up straight and walked quickly with a purpose. Farming activities helped keep him trim. Dad never wanted to join a senior-citizen group or admit to any part of aging. It was only in his last year that he let his hair grow to its natural shade of gray.

The Hondl granddaughters too have benefitted from Nadine's expertise. All four girls received their first haircuts from Aunt Nadine outdoors on the lawn at the farm or in the kitchen. In the 1980s when waves were all the rage, the granddaughters begged for and received crimped hairstyles. Niece Sara Thomasy, who has lived in California for more than a decade, has never had anyone else cut her hair even though that means she gets only one haircut a year when Aunt Nadine visits. A special family milestone occurred in 2013 when Sara's daughter, Charlotte Timberlake, at age 15 months, sat for her first trim with Great Aunt Nadine gently persuading her that it would not hurt.

Exploring the West with Grandchildren

In the 1980s, when their daughters were in grade school, Bernadette and Ken brought them from Ohio to Minnesota for a month-long stay on the farm in the summer. This was possible because Ken was a teacher and had summer vacation from school. Granddaughters Sara and Clare still say this was one of their favorite childhood experiences. They learned to bottle-feed calves and tame the barn cats and kittens. They explored the wetlands for frogs and took long walks to the bridge in the back field. Some evenings, the Thomasys and Grandma and Grandpa would all go for supper at The Place Restaurant in Blooming Prairie, Minnesota, and stop at a playground afterwards. Once the farm harvest was completed, the Thomasys took John with them on various western trips to Colorado, the Dakotas, Wyoming and Yellowstone National Park. They often visited at Colleen and Don's farm in southwest Minnesota on the way to and from their western destinations.

The 1988 trip to Yellowstone was probably Dad's and Bernadette's favorite. Although he had been to Yellowstone several times, he never tired of seeing Old Faithful and the steaming sulfur pits. He had a great time showing this amazing park to his daughter, son-in-law and granddaughters. He even agreed to take a bumpy stagecoach ride in Wyoming with Bernadette and her family. During these major trips, Mom unfortunately had to stay behind to take care of the farm, but she, Bernadette and the girls sometimes took a short trip to Red Wing, Minnesota, or the Amana Colonies in Iowa to give her a little vacation, too.

Sara Thomasy helps Grandpa John unload straw bales, summer 1986. After the straw harvest was completed, the family could go on vacation.

The Thomasys and John ride in the stagecoach in Yellowstone National Park in 1988. High in the rear seat are John, Sara and Ken; Bernadette and Clare in the second row, from right.

23

Moving On

Mom and Dad did not really retire. Instead they gradually moved to doing things differently. They continued with their beef cow herd until the late 1980s. Adaptations such as putting wheels on gates and designing a hay feeder that could be moved with a tractor made some farm tasks easier. The cows were all experienced by that time so calving was not such a big deal. Plus, the herd was considerably smaller. Dad continued to raise the calves but again things were done differently. A portable feed grinder helped. A trucker came to haul the fat cattle to market.

During the 1980s, Dad would often hire high school kids or other temporary workers to help with hay baling or to get other jobs such as harvest done. He had some favorites whom he called on often. We all remember one skinny young high school student who biked out from Owatonna one summer morning to help with hay baling. He was wearing shorts and had no hat or gloves. Neither Dad nor Mom thought he would last one day but surprisingly he turned out to be one of their most reliable and helpful workers for several years. If a worker showed any initiative, Dad would begin to take him under his wing, teaching him to do the work he needed done in a safe and efficient manner. Son-in-law Ken also was a big help for nine summers in the 1980s.

A Century Farm

In 1987, John and Dorothy's longtime farming efforts were rewarded when they achieved a major family milestone. The Hondl farm at 8161 Southeast 34th Avenue, Owatonna, Minnesota, was recognized as a Century Farm. The designation was presented by *The Farmer* magazine and the Minnesota State Fair for 100 years of continuous operation by the Hondl family. Beginning with Jan Hondl's purchase in 1881, carried forward by his son Anton and finally by John, the farm had grown and been improved with each generation. The entire family appreciated this honor and recognized its significance. It was a tribute not only to our parents, John and Dorothy, but also to the previous generations who had worked hard and valued the land.

This photo from the early 1980s shows John and Dorothy Hondl's farm site with all the new buildings and improvements made over the years. They received the Century Farm designation in 1987.

Mom and Dad remained actively involved in farming although most major planting and harvesting jobs were hired out. Dad continued to drive the tractors and even did some plowing in his early eighties. Farming ran deep in his veins and the call of the spring season kept a strong hold on him. Eventually in the 1990s all the cropland was rented out; a few years later the pasture and grassland also were rented. Even so, the proportions of cropland, pasture and grassland remained very similar to when Mom and Dad began farming over a half-century before. They continued living in the mobile home with the farmhouse also rented out. Dad still enjoyed talking farming with Kevin Christey, their land renter for many years, as well as Colleen's husband Don, who ran a large dairy operation with his brothers.

Mom was Dad's primary caregiver during his long battle with cancer and was deeply grieved when he passed away in 2002, as was his entire family. Dad had tried to prepare Mom for the future and advised her to buy a home in Owatonna so that she would have a safer place to live and more companionship during the winters. A few months later, she began a new life in a townhouse in north Owatonna where she could entertain friends and family and be close to shopping and services. Although it was emotional to leave the farm where she and Dad had lived and worked for sixty years, it proved to be a good move for her.

Mom continued handling the business of renting out the farmland and the house, as well as supervising small improvements and repairs. Mom inherited two large sheds full of machinery that was no longer needed since a renter was farming the land. She systematically had the machinery appraised and sold all of it piece by piece. Mom was quite satisfied with her efforts and held tough on several items to get fair prices from her buyers. Without the day-to-day farm responsibilities, Mom finally had the freedom to travel and socialize with local friends and relatives. She enjoyed going on bus trips with the Owatonna Senior Place group, joining card and garden clubs, and socializing. She especially enjoyed spending time with her sister, Mary, and her first cousin, Harriet Kubista Jirousek.

Passport to New Places

Mom was determined to do as much traveling as she could while she was able and, with help from her daughters, she did just that. In May 2004, Mom took her first overseas trip, flying from Detroit to Paris with Bernadette, Ken, Clare and Clare's friend Tiffany Snyder. They toured Monet's Gardens in Giverny, the beaches at Normandy, Mont St. Michel, numerous castles in the Loire Valley and of course Paris, where she enjoyed the Moulin Rouge, the Eiffel Tower and wonderful French food. Mom was the oldest

Dorothy in front of the Sacré-Coeur Basilica in the Montmartre district of Paris in 2004.

person in the tour group; fellow travelers called her the "Queen Mum." Mom worked hard not to slow the group down, and everyone looked out for her. They loved her enthusiasm, especially when she and another couple went to see the Parisian "can-can girls." It was reported that Dorothy had the most fun.

That December, Mom flew with Nadine to Costa Rica to celebrate Christmas with all the Thomasys, including Matt Timberlake, Sara's husband, who was our tour guide and driver. Matt and Sara arrived first and anxiously awaited the other two groups who had weather-related problems, flight changes and no cell phones to communicate. Since no one was at the airport to pick them up, Nadine and Mom bravely hired a taxi driver, who did not speak English, to take them the thirty miles to the lodge the family had reserved. Later that evening, Matt and Sara picked up Ken, Bernadette and Clare and drove them late at night on bumpy windy roads to the lodge. We still did not know if Mom and Nadine had even made it to Costa Rica. The next morning, it was a Christmas miracle when Sara and Clare heard Grandma's voice next door and realized that we were finally all together in the tropical paradise. Trip highlights included visiting a volcano, soaking in hot springs, zip-lining in the forest canopy (the young folks did, anyway), watching warm ocean waves, eating delicious tropical fruit, visiting a coffee plantation and a butterfly garden and bird-watching.

Another major trip for Nadine and Mom took them to the Canadian Rockies visiting Banff National Park in Alberta, Canada, as well as Glacier National Park in Montana. Mom enthusiastically tried all the extra excursions and had great times on a snow cat ride on the glaciers, her first helicopter ride and a river-rafting trip. Again, she amazed her tour mates with her willingness to try new experiences. Nadine's encouragement made these trips possible and very memorable for Mom.

Mom has traveled to four foreign countries and approximately twenty-two states. Her desire for going to new places remains strong. Mom loves being in the passenger seat for day trips to museums, gardens and scenic spots whenever she visits family in California or Minnesota.

24

Reflections on Our Czech and German Heritage

Growing up, we Hondl girls heard a great deal about our German heritage from Dad. It seemed as if the German part of it was emphasized while the Czech part was ignored. Our father may have promoted our German background because his father spoke German and he also spoke some. So, it was logical to associate one's heritage with the language spoken by one's parents. Dad carried through his interest in German by encouraging Colleen to take German when it was offered for the first time at Owatonna High School. Colleen was aghast to discover she was the only freshman girl in the class among many freshman boys. There were also many upperclassmen taking the course including a senior girl who became Homecoming Queen that fall. Intimidating to say the least! Dad and Colleen enjoyed comparing words; Dad spoke "low German" and Colleen was learning a more formal "high German." Still, the words were similar.

The Russian part of our history too was fascinating to think about as we grew up in the Cold War years. Colleen recalled trying to impress or perhaps shock grade school classmates with her "Russian relatives." She was right in that they were from Russia since they had lived on the Crimean Peninsula in Ukraine, but they were not Russian by heritage.

Even though it wasn't emphasized as we were growing up, it is also interesting to consider our Czech background. Czechs had over time been known as Bohemians since they were from the region of Bohemia. That term fell out of use sometime after World War I when the country of Czechoslovakia was established. There were other references including the not-so-nice slang version of Bohemians – "Bohunk" and the use of "bohemian," meaning a free or careless way of living or an unconventional person. Perhaps that is another reason why our Czech background was downplayed. We grew up knowing we were both Bohemian and German but not really recognizing that Bohemian meant

Czech. Nor did we realize how many of our neighbors and fellow Steele County residents also were Czech. It was the writing of this book years later that prompted us to delve more deeply into our heritage.

At times, it can be difficult to pick out what is truly Czech and what is really German both from an ancestral and cultural point of view. Our ancestors all listed Austria as their birthplace. That is largely due to the rule of the House of Hapsburg over the Austrian Empire and then after 1867, the Austro-Hungarian Empire, which included all the areas where our ancestors originated. Without going into details of a long and complicated history, it is important to note two facts. First, Bohemia and the surrounding areas were often caught between larger political and military forces sometimes making it a battleground. Second, there were a large number of Germans who moved into Bohemia. At times, the Germans and the Czechs lived peacefully together, complimenting each other with varied industrial and agricultural skills. At other times, though, political and religious preferences of the current rulers made for differences between the groups. Most likely Dad's ancestors were among those Germans who moved into Bohemia sometime between the 1600s to the 1800s, making him of German heritage.

On the cultural side, many of the food and everyday living practices were very similar and intertwined between Czechs and Germans. Yes, "kolaches," which are the homemade prune or poppy seed filled biscuits, are Czech in origin, but what about the from-scratch egg noodles Mom made? Where do they originate?

The Hondl daughters grew up with many Czech and German influences not realizing or appreciating what they were at the time. Many of the typical foods we made have been described earlier. But, foods such as sauerkraut, blood sausage and dumplings came from our heritage as did how we prepared meats, potatoes and vegetables. We enjoyed all of these foods but a less favored Czech tradition was the homemade cottage cheese. One step in the process was to hang a bag of cheese curds on the back of the kitchen stove's reservoir to allow it to drain and form. The cottage cheese was sometimes used in raisin biscuits making it more acceptable than eating it fresh.

Another way that our Czech heritage influenced us growing up was the emphasis on celebrating Easter. The Czech heritage places a lot of importance on Easter as a holiday. Czechs often brought in branches in the early spring to leaf out. Colleen continued that tradition in her own home bringing in lilac branches for Easter every year. Lilac branches were part of the decorations at her daughter Darielle's early spring wedding as well. The entire family also decorated Easter eggs by making a hole in either end of the egg, blowing out the contents and then dyeing them, something we did in our growing up years. In addition, Dad looked forward to Easter far more than Christmas as it signaled the start of a new growing season.

There was at least one place where both parts of our heritage came together. Both Czechs and Germans enjoy a good beer. Dad did too. The beer halls in the old country were somewhat re-created in places like the Monterey Ballroom south of Owatonna. But the beer hall was good for more than just drinking. Many of our relatives had their wedding dances or other special events there. Dances typically included polkas, schottisches and other dances with their origins in Eastern Europe. How fun it was for the kids to go sliding across the smooth, polished dance floor during intermissions.

The "old-time" music tradition carried over into our home too. On Sunday afternoons, we girls had to "endure" the music from KNUJ, the "polka station" from New Ulm, Minnesota. It was Dad's favorite. Mom continues to enjoy "old-time" accordion music.

In 1976, Nadine and Colleen went on a twenty-one day tour of Europe. One stop was the Hofbräuhaus in Munich, Germany. We were surprised to feel right at home with the old- time music playing as we were served potatoes, roast pork, dumplings and sauerkraut. Just like when we were growing up!

25

Farm Lessons and Who We Became

What influences made the biggest impressions on three daughters growing up on a livestock and grain farm in Steele County, Minnesota, in the late 1940s through the 1960s? Most likely it was a special combination of living close to the land and the hands-on nurturing by our parents. With the up-and-down weather, we came to appreciate how the family's livelihood depended on it. We learned quickly that farm work had to be the priority in daily life because the growing and selling of crops and livestock was how the bills got paid. As for the nurturing by our parents, they did not follow any books or take classes; they relied on their own family experience, gut instinct and practicality. In the rural environment, with minimal peer contact, we focused on our parents' guidance and teaching; they gave us a solid foundation for our teenage and adult years.

Dad treated us like boys and expected us to have confidence in ourselves. We learned how to drive tractors, back them up straight, hook up a wagon and make proper wide turns so what we were pulling would stay on the field road or, in some instances, the bridge on the field road. Bernadette, at age thirteen or fourteen, still remembers how nervous she was the first time she had to drive the big Dodge livestock truck across the narrow bridge on the back field road. "I had made this left turn many times with a tractor and wagon, so I took my time and successfully drove the truck loaded with soybeans over the bridge. To this day, I was surprised that Dad let me do this," Bernadette recalled. Dad, following behind with the combine, had no complaints with the result. It was a confidence building experience and good preparation for passing the first driver's license road test.

All of us daughters knew where to find tools and equipment in the "shop" in the machine shed. If we brought Dad the wrong item, we knew we would be sent back till we found the correct hammer, screwdriver or wrench. We learned the difference between a crescent wrench and a pipe wrench, a spike and a ten-penny nail, and knew a log chain when we saw one. This knowledge makes us all pretty handy with our own household repairs today. Bernadette, in particular, was Dad's right hand woman from a young age, fetching tools and helping to make repairs. When Dad was lying under the swather changing guards on the sickle, she would be handing him the bolts, washers, nuts, pliers or whatever he needed to make a repair.

Another value involved "making do." Both Mom and Dad instilled that in us. Mom encouraged us to use what we had in the kitchen to come up with something for supper. She also permitted us to do things like paint old furniture or re-arrange our rooms. Dad found a way to fix things even when he did not have quite the right part or the right tool. If we didn't have the newest machinery, we adapted what we had to make it work. In today's terms, we call that problem solving. It too is a product of our heritage and the times in which we grew up. But, it is carried forward in Mom and Dad's granddaughters. Colleen's daughter, Kim, has prided herself on being a good problem solver, often looking at what can be done if the first strategy doesn't work.

Mom and Dad worked hard to maintain a neat and tidy farm site and we daughters acquired that value as well. We put the German trait for neatness to work spring, summer and fall, pulling weeds, maintaining flowers beds, trimming shrubs, mowing the lawn and raking leaves. Even if it was dark when we returned from the field, we drove the tractors in the sheds and stored machinery inside—not only for neatness sake but because there was less chance of rust and damage occurring. Barn and other building doors were kept closed to prevent wind damage; gates were latched and fences kept in good repair to prevent livestock from getting out and making a mess.

There were so many ways our parents gave us responsibility, which fostered our independence and confidence from a young age through the teen years. At ages eight or ten, we were putting simple meals on the table. We helped with house cleaning and laundry, ran errands such as turning off the water at various tanks around the farm or carrying a lunchbox out to the field. Probably one of the most significant responsibilities given was having us take care of the farm and livestock while our parents went on week-long trips as depicted earlier. It was taken for granted that the farm and house would look neat and tidy just the way they left them when Mom and Dad returned. They expected that the animals would have been fed and watered as well. They trusted us to know when to call someone for assistance, if needed.

The strong role our mother played in the farm business was another factor that fostered us to become independent, self-sufficient adult women. While many farm wives at that time did not handle financial responsibilities, our mother did. In our house, it was the norm for Mom to keep records, file taxes, go to the bank, write checks and pay bills. Some of this occurred because Mom had more education than Dad; however, other husbands in the 1950s might not have had the trust or humility to allow their wives to handle financial matters.

Throughout this family history, we have mentioned our Uncle Clement, Dad's older brother who lived with our family for more than thirty years. This experience impressed on us daughters the importance of family loyalty, responsibility and unselfishness. Out of compassion for Clement, who suffered from mental illness, our father gave him a place to live and our mother did her best to help welcome Clement and his sometimes unsocial behavior to the household. Due to minimal mental health services at the time, his condition was never diagnosed nor treated. Clement worked alongside Dad and Mom and was a genuine member of our family. As we girls got older, we kept his room clean and did his laundry. Uncle Clement shared meals with us, celebrated holidays and birthdays, worked in the fields, fed the livestock and lived as productive a life as possible outside an institution.

Because of Uncle Clement's unpredictable behavior, however, we girls did not bring our friends to the farm as often as we would have liked. Dad was concerned about how Clement might react to strangers. As teenagers, we would have been embarrassed to have our friends see our uncle laughing at odd times and carrying on a conversation with himself. Looking back now, this was a small price for us girls to pay. We came to realize the enormity of what our parents did to give our Uncle Clement a good home and quality of life. Clement lived continuously on the Hondl farm until 1974, when after a short stay in a nursing home, he died of cancer at age sixty-five.

For the Hondl girls, many of these values imparted by our parents and our life on the farm influenced both what we chose to do in life and how we did it.

Nadine

As I grew up on the farm, I realized that nothing was going to be given to me. So I was encouraged to work on my 4-H projects and get rewarded in a different way. One of my high points was winning a grand champion ribbon at the Steele County Fair in a horticulture and gardening project. I planted and tended my first flower garden and picked flowers from it for the purple ribbon award. After that, the passion to work hard to try to win more awards and do well was instilled in me for life.

In high school, I felt that I had three career choices: dress designer, florist and hairdresser. However, I was directed into the business track in high school, which gave me a lot of anxiety because I had to try to do well at shorthand, typing and bookkeeping. I also took courses in art and home economics, which I enjoyed and excelled at. One of my proudest accomplishments was the "A" I earned in home economics for a spring dress coat I sewed. Another high point was winning a poster contest sponsored by Owatonna merchants in 1960.

According to Mom, my interest in hairdressing goes back a long ways. She says that when I was just a toddler, I would sit on top of Dad's chest gently combing his hair while he napped. Since I had been setting and occasionally cutting my sisters' and mother's hair for several years, it did not surprise my family and friends when I enrolled in the cosmetology program at Austin Area Vocational School a few days after high school graduation. There I received the basic training for a very satisfying, long-time career in hairdressing. But my career would not have gone far had I not applied some of the values I learned on the farm: the patience to grow and be responsible to build a clientele through endurance and professional knowledge. After sixteen years of successful work at Ramseth's Salon in Austin, Minnesota, I moved to Minneapolis, where I built up a loyal group of clients primarily during thirty-two years at Peppertree Salon in New Hope and later at Plaza Salon in Plymouth. I enjoyed the challenges of the business side of the profession and had my mother's confidence in handling the financial aspects of it.

As I reached my seventies, I realized that my farm background, with its emphasis on perseverance and working smart, has paid off. I still enjoy gardening, hairdressing and home decorating. My father John never used the word "retire" and I, too, am avoiding that word.

Bernadette

Throughout our grade school and high school years, Dad instilled in us daughters the importance of "getting our schooling," something he lacked and felt stigmatized about many times during his life. He and Mom, too, wanted better for their daughters. Their decision to send us to Catholic grade school put us on the track to accomplish these goals – far beyond their expectations. They did not just tell us to succeed; they provided us with the school setting in which we could learn the most. I chose the college-prep course of study at Owatonna High School, where the benefit of encouraging teachers and the help of scholarships enabled me to attend the University of Minnesota.

As the picture below shows, it was an emotional and milestone day when we packed our '57 DeSoto with my three suitcases, portable typewriter, and a few belongings and headed for Minneapolis and the university campus. Dad even wore a suit for the occasion. The typewriter was my high school graduation gift. I always remember that my parents gave it to me early because Dad could not wait for me to open it. The day I left for college I also took with me valuable lessons learned on the Hondl farm: work hard, don't give up and be responsible for yourself. Four years later, I received a Bachelor's degree in English education and was the first in the extended Hondl family to graduate from college.

The Hondl family prepares to take Bernadette to the University of Minnesota in Minneapolis in 1962. The photo appeared in *Reminisce Extra*, September 2014.

Like my Dad, I really wanted to make it on my own and my goal was to leave Minnesota. I taught high school English in Port Huron, Michigan for two years, then earned a Master's degree in journalism at the University of Michigan in Ann Arbor. I worked as a newspaper reporter at *The Blade* in Toledo, Ohio, for nine years, meanwhile meeting my husband Ken Thomasy. We raised two daughters in the Toledo area, and I continued working there in the journalism/marketing/public relations field for more than twenty-five years. A few years after retiring, my husband and I followed our daughters to California where they were starting careers. We have lived there since 2009.

As we were growing up, Dad often reminded us of the importance of time management or in farm terms "to make hay while the sun shines." This practice too was a key to success in my career and is one that still works for me today. Getting up early, doing the most important work right away and not wasting time are attitudes I learned on the farm and have tried to instill in my family. Those early mornings of getting up to load cattle for market or summer afternoons spent baling hay instead of going to Kohlmeier Beach left an indelible impression on me. And, like my mother, I pay the bills and take care of the financial matters for my family.

Colleen

As the youngest in the family, I had a little bit different growing-up experience from that of my older sisters. Most likely I was able to do more things in school, such as participating in more extracurricular activities and gatherings with friends. Still, I grew up with a sense of duty that was instilled in me by my parents. I learned that if I said I was going to do something, then I had better do it. Following through on things and being committed were important values to me.

I loved animals, and so Dad and I talked about what it might be like to be a veterinarian. Reality hit early in my college years. Although I liked chemistry, it really was not my strong suit. My grade point average probably would not have gotten me into veterinary school. Also, I had so many interests that it was hard to decide on an area to pursue; I was kind of all over the place. I actually started out in political science in the honors program at the University of Minnesota. Eventually, because I liked chemistry and clothing construction, I decided on the textile science track in home economics. However, it was not a realistic major in terms of getting a job. As a result, during my senior year I took a wide range of electives to round out my background and to give me a better chance of landing a position with the Extension Service, which is an outreach arm of state land grant universities with a presence in every county in the United States.

That career choice took me to southwest Minnesota where I worked in Cottonwood and Nobles counties, primarily with home economics responsibilities and later in Murray County with 4-H Youth Development. Although I worked in rural counties, my responsibilities were never limited to working with farm families. However, my farm background was helpful as I worked with professionals and the community during the farm crisis of the 1980s.

Marrying a farmer wasn't something I set out to do, but it did happen! I met Don Gengler while working in Cottonwood County. He was a dairy farmer, which was interesting in that my parents had quit milking cows the year I was born. However, a one-family dairy farm like many of our neighbors had, was quite a bit different from a large one in which three brothers worked together as Don's family did. It made life much more flexible and workable. The values of independence and taking responsibility as well as my farm background certainly came into play in my home life. If Don was gone to work at the dairy, I could take care of most house and yard chores and make simple repairs.

Those same values carried over into my professional career for all the time I worked in Extension. I continued working in Extension with a variety of responsibilities from 1988 to 2003, when I worked part time to allow myself more family time. In 2004, Extension became a regional system, meaning that I had statewide responsibilities. I retired in 2012 after thirty-eight years with Extension but continue to work part time in coordinating professional development in southwest Minnesota.

Love of the Land

We know our growing up years on the farm fostered a deep love of the land in all three of us. We fondly recall our family getting in the car or truck on a summer evening and taking a drive up the road to admire the crops and rejoice in the miracle that sun, seed, soil and rain could produce. Sixty years later, we still get excited in the spring when the first tractors and diggers begin to crisscross the fields. Although Nadine and

Bernadette left the farm to live city lives, they still keep close tabs on the farm growing seasons and love to see the fields turning green with new corn and soybean plants in arrow straight rows. When she isn't working in her own gardens, Nadine makes frequent trips to the Hondl farm in the summer and fall to plant flowers, trim shrubs and rake leaves. Colleen, also an avid gardener, and her husband Don assist Mom with farm business management. Nadine and Bernadette also love visiting Colleen and Don's farm near Iona, Minnesota, where Colleen continues to enjoy the best of both worlds. She lives on the farm where she raised her family while she continues to work part time for Extension, a career that over the years took her to cities and towns throughout Minnesota.

Bernadette still remembers enjoying a farm publication that her parents used to read called *The Land*. Its cover always featured a photo of a beautiful rural landscape. Any one of those photos could easily have been taken on our farm – the Hondl land – in Aurora Township, Steele County, Minnesota.

26

The Next Generation

One-hundred-fifty years after their ancestors from Bohemia arrived in America, the Hondl daughters are confident that these family pioneers would be very proud of what the current generation is accomplishing now. Not only do the four granddaughters share and uphold many of the valued traditions of their forebears, they also are developing new paths in order to thrive in a complex future.

Carrying on the 4-H Tradition

Bernadette and Colleen both encouraged their daughters to participate in the 4-H program because it was such an important part of their growing-up years. All four granddaughters followed in the 4-H tradition. Sara and Clare Thomasy lived in the city (suburban Toledo, Ohio), but their mother found a way to give them some of the same 4-H experiences she had enjoyed. When Sara, at about age 10, developed a strong interest in horses, the Thomasys joined the Anthony Wayne Trailblazers 4-H Club, a group that focused on equine projects. Sara, and Clare too, began with the horseless horse project to gain general knowledge. Sara, eventually competed in Western and English style riding events and spent summers working and training at Peg and Ben Brown's Walnut Hill Farm, where the Thomasys leased a horse for her to ride. These experiences, no doubt, furthered Sara's interest in becoming a veterinarian. Both Sara and Clare took additional 4-H projects, including creative writing and environmental science. Clare later found her sport in competitive swimming, rather than horseback riding, but she continued with 4-H. She was a 4-H camp counselor and took food, nutrition and photography projects. Both girls competed at the county level and at the Ohio State Fair. Clare also participated in the Citizenship-Washington Focus trip to Washington, DC.

Kim and Darielle Gengler also were very active in 4-H. They probably did not have a choice! Their mother was working with 4-H Youth Development at the time as part of her job with the University of

Minnesota Extension. The girls first joined the Lucky Aces of Iona 4-H Club and later on, the Mason Hustlers 4-H Club. Kim especially enjoyed the projects which made use of her creativity including photography, creative arts and home environment. She showed dairy cattle as well. Darielle took food and nutrition projects, photography and clothing which by then covered both constructed and purchased clothing. Every summer, she did a clothing inventory which would justify that summer's purchase for a fair exhibit. She too showed dairy cattle. They each won trips to the Minnesota State Fair. Both girls served as County 4-H Ambassadors helping with events and promoting the 4-H program. Kim was a 4-H camp counselor and Darielle attended the Citizenship-Washington Focus trip to Washington, DC. In retrospect, both girls would like to have taken advantage of each of those opportunities, but all in all, they appreciated their time in the 4-H program.

Kim Gengler leads her 4-H entry before the judges at the Murray County Fair, 1998.

Darielle Gengler gets her heifer ready to show at the 1998 4-H Dairy Show, Murray County Fair.

Looking for a Minnesota Sky

Sara and Clare came to cherish another family tradition from their visits to the Hondl farm in the 1980s. Their mother Bernadette loved the deep blue Minnesota sky when it was filled with puffy, white clouds. She often pointed out these scenes to her daughters and, when they were back in Ohio, Sara and Clare would sometimes notice a similarly lovely sky and say, "It's a Minnesota sky." Colleen's daughters also grew up with special admiration for this Minnesota phenomenon. An avid photographer from her 4-H days, Colleen would grab her camera and tell her daughters that it was "a good cloud day." In other words, "a Minnesota sky" filled with amazing white clouds was waiting to be captured on film. Both Kim and Darielle loved the challenge of taking photos with those beautiful settings. To this day, all the granddaughters, no matter where they live, continue to look for and appreciate "a Minnesota sky."

College and Careers

The granddaughters grew up each following their own interests. Sara Thomasy, DVM, PhD, is a veterinarian specializing in ophthalmology. She works at the University of California Davis School of Veterinary Medicine. Sara lives in Sacramento, California, with her husband Matt Timberlake and their daughter Charlotte Foushee Timberlake. Clare Thomasy, OD, is a Managing Optometrist with Eyexam of California, currently working in Sacramento. Clare practiced in the San Francisco Bay area for four years before returning to Sacramento. Kimberly Gengler moved to the San Francisco Bay area right after college graduation for a position in publishing. She now lives and works in San Francisco; she currently is a Senior Public Relations Manager at Riverbed Technology. Darielle Gengler-Hanson is a Staffing Specialist working with interns for Target Corporation headquartered in Minneapolis. She and her husband, Isaac McGurran-Hanson, live in Richfield, Minnesota.

We look forward to the new chapters this next generation will write in our family history. Three of the granddaughters have followed their great grandfather's footsteps and are living and working in California, while the youngest appreciates all that Minnesota has to offer. All four women are exploring their world by traveling and looking for new opportunities, just as their immigrant ancestors did when they left the small villages in Bohemia in Eastern Europe more than a century and a half ago.

27

Postscript - A Visit to the Homeland

A logical step in writing about our memories of growing up and exploring our family history is to journey to where our ancestors once lived. Colleen was fortunate to be able to do that in the summer of 2014. She and her husband Don traveled to the villages of Dlouhá Třebová, Rudoltice and Ribnick in the Pardubice Region of the Czech Republic.

Colleen and her husband Don are welcomed by city officials in Dlouhá Třebová, Czech Republic in 2014.

All three villages are part of our great-grandparents' histories. The Kubistas on Dorothy's side of the family were from Dlouhá Třebová, now a thriving and impressive village of just over 1200. Just a few miles away is Ribnick, a smaller village of about 800. At one time, it may have been one of the German-speaking villages located in that region and it is where the German side of our family comes from. John's maternal grandparents, John Haubenschild and Frances Groh, were born in Ribnick. Later, they were married in Rudoltice, just eight miles away. It is amazing to think that our great-grandparents on both sides of the family came from neighboring villages but most likely did not know each other in the "old country." Even in Steele County in the late 19th and early 20th century, people stayed within their small communities. It is only later that people gained more mobility.

To have parents each with origins in the same small geographic area of the Czech Republic is quite remarkable. The blending together of the Czech and German cultures from each side of the family, as it occurred in these small villages, was confusing to us at first, but now, after some study, makes sense. Our father, who emphasized our German heritage, did not have the historical background to provide us with these explanations.

It takes some time to think about what the journey to the villages meant. Was it only about learning what the land of our ancestors looked like? Was it trying to understand why they left? Was it thinking about what their lives would have been like had they not come to the United States? Indeed, it is all those things and more.

Dlouhá Třebová village crest; European cities of all sizes have a crest.

The land is beautiful around the Czech villages and felt like the Minnesota home of our growing up years. It is a little more rolling there, with a few more trees, but the new country must have felt right to our long-ago relatives as they settled here. However, the feeling of home would have been secondary to them. They needed the land for its ability to successfully support their families. The Hondls, the Haubenschilds, the Kubistas and the Spindlers lacked for opportunity in their homeland. For example, if a son was not first-born, he would not inherit the land. How was he to make a living? The United States, with its abundant land available to homesteaders with only minimal requirements, must have looked very promising.

On our trip, we heard a great deal about the history of the Czech Republic from the time of Charles IV in the 14th century to the height of the Austro-Hungarian Empire in the mid-to-late 19th century, at which time many of our ancestors left to live in the United States. Over hundreds of years, Bohemia was a region between large, aggressive empires, countries and peoples. Bohemia was sometimes a buffer between those, a land to be bargained with, or an area to be claimed because of the people who had settled there decades or even centuries earlier. How strong those Czechs were to survive all of that. So too were the Germans who moved into Bohemia and lived there for centuries. Their industrious, adaptable and proud nature served them well as they immigrated to the United States, enduring hardships we can only imagine.

We learned much about what the Czechs experienced during the two World Wars and the years of Communist rule from 1948 to 1989. On our visit to the villages, we hired a car and driver. The black Mercedes driven by a young man in white shirt and tie prompted some interested looks from villagers not unlike what might happen in a small town in Minnesota. However, one experience was far different. We were going down a steep hill next to the cemetery in Dlouhá Třebová. Traveling up the hill on the other side of the road was a farm combine followed by an older woman on foot. As soon as she saw our car, she stopped, looked downward submissively and stayed motionless until we were past. The experience left a big impression on us. In our own small town we might be curious about a strange vehicle, but we would not fear it. This woman's years of living under oppression was still taking its toll even after twenty-five years of freedom.

Dorothy visits marker where her grand-parents, Ignac and Rosalie Kubista, are buried.

The writing of these stories and exploring our family history has been an eye opener for all three Hondl daughters and our mother too. Did we accomplish what we set out to do? We recorded stories from our mother and father as well as our own stories. We reflected on the responsibilities we were given as we grew up and what that meant for us as adults. We discovered names and dates of family members several generations back. We studied the history of the homeland of our ancestors and one of us traveled there. Although we did not have letters or diaries to tell us what our ancestors were thinking and feeling, we still came to a much better sense of what our heritage is through this journey.

We believe that our ancestors from Bohemia were looking for better lives and broader opportunities for the future generations. No doubt they would be proud of what the next generation is doing now. All four granddaughters are college graduates, two with advanced degrees, and are successfully pursuing their lives and careers.

A few weeks after the trip, Colleen took her mother Dorothy to the HRBITOV-SV-VACLAVA (St. Wenceslaus Cemetery), better known in Steele County as the Saco Cemetery. As we stood by the headstone of Mom's grandparents, Ignac and Rosalie Kubista, we thought about the huge distance they had come and the barriers they encountered. What courage and pluck they must have had! For Colleen, it was significant to think of visiting the cemetery in Dlouhá Třebová with the Kubista family plot and then seeing the Kubista name on the headstone at Saco Cemetery. Similar sentiments could be said for all of the branches in our family tree.

We three daughters are thankful for our life in the United States. At the same time, we recognize, admire and revere those distant fourth and fifth cousins who may still be in the villages of Dlouhá Třebová, Ribnick or other parts of the Czech Republic. Colleen did not find long-lost relatives on her trip, but perhaps that is still in our future.

Appendix A:

The Anton J. and Lena Hondl Family

Helen   b. 1902, d. 1975,
          m. Walter Renchin _____ , b. 1896, d. 1972
     Children – Walter Jr., b. 1927, d. 1999

Benita   b. 1903, d. 1962,
          m. John Ressler _____ , b. 1892, d. 1968
     Children – Clement, b. 1922, d. 1988; Dorothy, b. 1925, d. 2011;
     Lloyd, b. 1931, d. 1978; DeeAnn

Clarence   b. 1905, d. 1974,
          m. Helen Johnson Oct. 15, 1930,
     Children – George; Donald; Richard; Deloris

Myrtle   b. 1908, d. 1984,
          m. Anton Ressler _____, b. 1893, d. 1984
     Children – Donald, b. 1925; Margie, b. 1927; Luvern, b. 1929

Clement   b. 1909, d. 1974

John   b. 1912, d. 2002,
          m. Dorothy Spindler Nov. 26, 1941, b. 1920
     Children – Nadine, b. 1943; Bernadette, b. 1944; Colleen, b. 1951

Loretta   b. 1913, d. 1984,
          m. Richard Haberman Oct. 1934, b. 1912, d. 1967
     Children – DeWayne, Tom, Katherine

George   b. 1915, d. 1964,
          m. Louise Christiansen June 15, 1937,
          b. 1919, d. 1954
     Children – Darrell, Karen, LaRaine, Marlen, b. 1949, d. 1954

Appendix B:

The Frank J. and Agnes J. Spindler Family

Helen   b. 1899, d. 1980,
     m. Anton Kubista Sept. 28, 1920,
     b. 1895, d. 1964
   Children – Irene, b. 1924; Jerome, b. 1926; George;
   Bernard, b. 1931

William   b. 1902, d. 1978,
     m. Agnes Deml Oct. 24, 1944,
     b. 1915, d. 2008
   Children – Suzanne, Myron, Leo, Dennis, Bill, Therese

Charles   b. 1904, d. 1996,
     m. Bertha Schrom 1929, b. 1905, d. 2004
   Children – Lawrence, b. 1927, d. 2010; Bobby, b. 1929, d. 1933;
   Bernice, b. 1935, d. 2005; Dolores, b. 1937, d. 1992;
   Rita, b. 1939

Frank   b. 1907, d. 1983,
     m. Irene Warner about 1931, b.1913, d. 1995
   Children – Eugene, b. 1932; Luverne, b. 1933;
   Paul, b. 1935, d. 2009; Rosemary, b. 1936; Walter, Duane

Agnes   b. 1910, d. 1935,
     m. Richard Sommer Oct. 1, 1930,
     b. 1905, d. 1988
   Children – Bernita; Annette, d. 2014

Roselyn   b. 1913, d. 2005,
     m. Edward Schrom 1931, b. 1910, d. 1993
   Children – Marcella, b. 1932; Harriet, b. 1934; Norbert, b. 1937;
   Audrey, b. 1939; Roger, b. 1951, d. 2005; Craig

John   b. 1915, d. 2008,
            m. Sylvia Fisher Nov. 7, 1939,
            b. 1918, d. 2008
    Children – Beatrice, Elaine, Karen, Urban, Louise

Mary   b. 1918, d. 2007,
            m. Edward Warner Nov. 20, 1940
            b. 1916, d. 2005
    Children – Kenneth, b. 1941; Shirley, b. 1945; Diane, b. 1953

Dorothy   b. 1920,
            m. John Hondl Nov. 26, 1941
            b. 1912, d. 2002
    Children – Nadine, b. 1943; Bernadette, b. 1944;
            Colleen, b. 1951

Appendix C:

The John F. and Dorothy S. Hondl Family

Nadine   b. 1943,

Bernadette   b. 1944,
       m. Kenneth Thomasy Aug. 13, 1971, b. 1942
   Children: –Sara, b. 1979, m. Matthew Timberlake
        Aug. 3, 2003, b. 1977
        Child – Charlotte, b. 2011
      – Clare, b. 1981

Colleen   b. 1951,
       m. Donald Gengler Dec. 9, 1978, b. 1949
   Children:– Kimberly, b. 1983
      – Darielle, b. 1988, m. Isaac McGurran- Hanson
        April 6, 2013, b. 1987

Note: more family genealogy is available at Ancestry.Com, Hondl Family Tree, http://trees.ancestry.com/tree/70766491/family

Appendix D:

Alternative spellings:
Names

- Ignac for Ignatz (Ignac Kubista – Dorothy's maternal grandfather)
- Rosa, also Rosalia, Roselie and Rosie; Basharna, also Pisorna and Teshorna (Rosa Basharna – Dorothy's maternal grandmother). Names appear differently in various sources including on her grave marker and in her obituary.
- Frank for Franz, also Frantisek (Frank W. Spindler – Dorothy's paternal grandfather; her father was Frank Joseph Spindler)
- Frances for Franzes (Frances Groh – John's maternal grandmother)
- John for Jan (Jan Hondl – John's paternal grandfather)
- Haubenschild, also Haubenschield, Howbenschild, Haubenchild and Hobenschield (John Haubenschild – John's maternal grandfather). Names appear differently in various sources including on his grave marker and in his obituary.

Places

Krym. Today known as the Crimean Peninsula

Ribnick, also Rybnik, Ribnica. There are many towns and villages called "Ribnick" which in Czech has the generic meaning of "fish pond." In trying to establish which Ribnick John's maternal grandparents (John Haubenschild and Frances Groh) came from, it is almost certain that it is the Ribnick located in the Ústí and Orlicí District of the Pardubice Region of the present day Czech Republic. This village is approximately eight and half miles from Rudoltice where the two were married. The short distance has been verified.

Other Hondl, Spindler and Kubista relatives were from towns and villages in this region of the present day Czech Republic as are many of the Czech immigrants in Steele County. Some of those towns and villages in the Ústí and Orlicí District include: Česká Třebová, Dlouhá Třebová, Dobříkov, Dolní Čermná, Dolní Dobrouč, Dolní Morava, Rudoltice and Rybník.

Rudoltice. Czech spelling, German spelling is Rudelsdorf.

Appendix E:

Highlights of Farm and Home Improvements and Modernization

1918 – Large square addition of five bedrooms, living and dining rooms was built onto the tiny original farmhouse, which originally had only a kitchen, two upstairs bedrooms, a pantry and a cellar. The new addition featured dormers on the attic and a long porch with pillars across the front.

1925 – The current barn was built at a cost of $8,000. Two earlier barns were both destroyed by fire. The latter one, insured for $2,000, caught fire during threshing. A 16 x 38-foot block silo also was constructed soon after.

1930s – Tiling of some farmland was completed by Anton Hondl.

1941 – John Hondl bought the farm's first tractor, a used McCormick Deering, purchased with a $150 loan from his future wife Dorothy.

1947 – Electricity was installed in the house, barn and chicken coop. Waterworks system was also installed on the farm but not yet to the house.

1948 – John Hondl bought the first set of large Goodyear Super-Grip tractor tires in Steele County, enabling him to get through "100 acres of wet, soggy, tough-to-whip soil," according to an article in the Steele County Photo News.[22]

1949 – A second silo was built beside the first block silo.

1951 – John paid $5,400 for one of the first combines in Steele County. This Massey-Harris Model 27 machine and others like it eventually made threshing machines obsolete.

1951 – John and Dorothy quit their dairy operation and began beef production, which continued until the late 1980s.

1952 – After renting on shares for ten years, John and Dorothy Hondl purchased the farm from the Lena Hondl estate. In spite of bad economic times on the farm they were able to build both a large corn crib and a 100-foot Quonset style machine shed that year.

1952 – Windbreaks of evergreens and arbor vitae trees were planted on the south side and along the roadside.

1956 – Cattle shed and feed lot were constructed south of the barn. Construction crews removed soil from the field hill east of the home site to raise and level the area needed for the feedlot and shed.

1956 – A waterline was connected to the house. A single faucet was installed in the large, washboard style sink; it ran cold water only.

1959 – Time for improvements on the house. The old south-side porch was torn off and replaced with a one-car garage and new entrance to the kitchen. The kitchen was remodeled and a bathroom added off the kitchen. The exterior of the older section of the house was covered with white aluminum siding and eventually the entire house was sided with aluminum. Also, a new furnace was installed and radiators repaired so we could again use the hot water system.

1966 – Woven wire fence was put around the entire pasture to hold heifers purchased to start a beef herd.

1968 – Dormers were removed from the house to reduce heat loss; new roof was installed. The front porch was re-done with the plank flooring replaced with a cement patio. Timbers replaced the old wooden columns.

1974 – One of the oldest buildings, the granary, was torn down to make way for a new steel grain-storage and machine shed. No one was sorry to see the granary go because setting up the elevator to store grain there was one of the most frustrating annual tasks on the farm.

1974 – In the fall, a three-bedroom mobile home was installed just south of the main house. John and Dorothy moved into it so that a renter family could live in the main house. It was a way for the Hondls to lighten the load of farming while still keeping a hand in the operation and living on the farm they loved and built up over the years.

1979 – A second steel machine shed was built north of the driveway.

1985 – The two block silos, which had not been used for some time, were removed.

1985 – Barn re-roofed with steel.

1987 – The Hondl farm received the Century Farm designation as recognized by *The Farmer* magazine and the Minnesota State Fair. To qualify, farms must be at least fifty acres and be in continuous family ownership for at least 100 years.

2003 – Mobile home removed after Dorothy purchased a townhouse and moved to Owatonna.

2005 – Additional tiling was completed on the land east of the bridge. The field road, which had previously run between the northern-most field and led out to the grassland known as "the prairie," was eliminated making one large field.

2009 – New windows, vinyl siding and insulation installed on farmhouse.

Notes

1. Joan Groh, "Groh Family," Geneaology.com, accessed January 5, 2014, http://familytreemaker.genealogy.com/users/g/r/o/Joan-Groh-Montana/PDFBOOK1.pdf, 2.

2. Franklyn Curtiss-Wedge, History of Rice and Steele Counties Minnesota, vol. 2. (Chicago, H. C. Cooper Jr., 1910), 1240.

3. "Ellendale Roundup," The People's Press, December 30, 1910, accessed February 7, 2014, http://newspapers.mnhs.org/web/mhsnews/web/imu.php?request=multimedia&irn=10371049&format=pdf&kind=supplementary

4. Joan Groh, "Groh Family," 8.

5. U.S. Census Bureau, "12th Census of the United States: 1900," Minnesota, Steele County, Aurora Township Enumerations District 123, accessed March 24, 2014, from interactive.ancestry.com, 6.

6. Ibid., 6.

7. Curtiss-Wedge, History of Rice, 1145-1146.

8. Angela Mary Bureau, Family Tree of František Kubišta I and Anna Šouba. Theos Books, 2000.

9. Michael Wolesky, We Lack for Nothing Now: Czech Settlement in Steele County, Minnesota (Wolindoo, 2011), 106-107.

10. "Death of Ignac Kubista," The People's Press, April 17, 1914, Section 2, accessed February 6, 2014, http://newspapers.mnhs.org/web/mhsnews/web/imu.php?request=multimedia&irn=10378869&format=pdf&kind=supplementary

11. "Obituary Mrs. Rosie Kubista," Owatonna Journal Chronicle, July 2, 1915, Volume LV (55), Issue #27, Page 7, Column 4.

12. "Machine Serial Numbers: Two Letter Prefix," Singer Sewing Company, accessed February 13, 2015, http://www.singerco.com/support/machine-serial-numbers/double-letter

13. "Western Equine Encephalomyelitis," Los Angeles County West Vector & Vector-Borne Disease Control District, accessed February 10, 2015, http://www.lawestvector.org/wee.htm

14. Wendy Reuer, "Lecture series focuses on POW camp in Owatonna," Owatonna People's Press, March 24, 2009, accessed August 31, 2014, http://www.southernminn.com/owatonna_peoples_press/archives/articl e_08157490-cb82-5857-bb0e-b37df66eb65f.html

15. "Goodyear Tires Go Through," PN Photo, Steele County Photo News, January 8, 1948.

16. University of Minnesota Department of Agriculture and United States Department of Agriculture, Annual Report of the Southeastern Minnesota Farm Management Service, no. 195, (St. Paul, Minnesota, Division of Agricultural Economics, 1951), http://ageconsearch.umn.edu/bitstream/13110/1/mr520195.pdf, 20.

17. "Kernie's offered fine dining and entertainment in Ellendale," Owatonna People's Press, November 6, 2004, accessed on September 8, 2014, http://www.southernminn.com/owatonna_peoples_press/archives/articl e_47573e96-38c8-5b37-947d-b774c17780c8.html.

18. University of Minnesota Department of Agriculture and United States Department of Agriculture, Annual Report of the Southeastern Minnesota Farm Management Service, no. 114, (St. Paul, Minnesota, Division of Agricultural Economics, 1939),

http://ageconsearch.umn.edu/bitstream/13104/1/mr400114.pdf, 14.

19. School District Consolidations, History of Consolidation, Minnesota House of Representatives, House Research Department, accessed on February 13, 2014, http://www.house.leg.state.mn.us/hrd/issinfo/schdistcon.aspx?src=7#Year

20. Cobbett Steinberg, TV Facts (Facts on File, Inc, 1980), accessed October 11, 2014 from Television History: The First 75 Years: http://www.tvhistory.tv/Annual_TV_Households_50-78.JPG.

21. "Kernels – Bits of rural wisdom, wit and wonder . . . gleaned from here and there," Farm and Ranch Living, June/July 1987, Vol. 10, No. 2, 20.

22. "Goodyear Tires Go Through." Steele County Photo News.

Bibliography

Bureau, Angela Mary. *Family Tree of František Kubišta I and Anna Šouba.* Theos Books, 2000.

Curtiss-Wedge, Franklyn. *History of Rice and Steele Counties Minnesota,* vol. 2. Chicago: H. C. Cooper Jr., 1910.

"Death of Ignac Kubista." *The People's Press,* April 17, 1914, Section 2. Accessed February 6, 2015. http://newspapers.mnhs.org/web/mhsnews/web/imu.php?request=multimedia&irn=10378869&format=pdf&kind=supplementary

Descendants of Johann Haubenschild – Updated for Family Reunion. *Geneaology.com.* Accessed January 3, 2014. http://familytreemaker.genealogy.com/users/h/a/u/Gordon-J-Haubenschild/ODT6-0001.html

"Ellendale Roundup." *The People's Press,* December 30, 1910. Accessed February 7, 2015. http://newspapers.mnhs.org/web/mhsnews/web/imu.php?request=multimedia&irn=10371049&format=pdf&kind=supplementary

"Goodyear Tires Go Through." PN Photo. *The Steele County Photo News,* January 8, 1948.

Groh, Joan. "Groh Family." Geneaology.com. Accessed January 5, 2014. http://familytreemaker.genealogy.com/users/g/r/o/Joan-Groh Montana/PDFBOOK1.pdf

"History Center: Butter Capital of the World." *Eventful.* Accessed September 24, 2014. http://eventful.com/owatonna/events/history-center-butter-capital-world-/E0-001-049641272-8

Hupchick, Dennis P., and Harold E. Cox. *The Palgrave Concise Historical Atlas of Eastern Europe.* New York: Palgrave, 2001.

"Kernels – Bits of rural wisdom, wit and wonder . . . gleaned from here and there." *Farm and Ranch Living*, June/July 1987, Vol. 10, No. 2.

"Kernie's offered fine dining and entertainment in Ellendale." *Owatonna People's Press*, November 6, 2004.
http://www.southernminn.com/owatonna_peoples_press/archives/article_47573e96-38c8-5b37-947d-b774c17780c8.html

"Machine Serial Numbers: Two Letter Prefix." Singer Sewing Company. Accessed February 13, 2015.
http://www.singerco.com/support/machine-serial-numbers/double-letter

"Obituary Mrs. Rosie Kubista." *Owatonna Journal Chronicle*, July 2, 1915, Volume LV (55), Issue #27.

Reuer, Wendy. "Lecture series focuses on POW camp in Owatonna." *Owatonna People's Press*, March 24, 2009.
http://www.southernminn.com/owatonna_peoples_press/archives/article_08157490-cb82-5857-bb0e-b37df66eb65f.html

School District Consolidations, History of Consolidation. Minnesota House of Representatives, House Research Department. Accessed on February 13, 2014.
http://www.house.leg.state.mn.us/hrd/issinfo/schdistcon.aspx?src=7#Year

Sprinclova Choy, Leona. *Czeching My Roots – A Heritage Saga & Autobiography*. Winchester, Virginia: Golden Morning Publishing, 2002.

Steinberg, Cobbett. *TV Facts*. Facts on File, Inc, 1980. Accessed October 11, 2014 from Television History: The First 75 Years.
http://www.tvhistory.tv/Annual_TV_Households_50-78.JPG

University of Minnesota Department of Agriculture and United States Department of Agriculture. *Annual Report of the Southeastern Minnesota*

Farm Management Service, no. 114. St. Paul, Minnesota: Division of Agricultural Economics, 1939. http://ageconsearch.umn.edu/bitstream/13104/1/mr400114.pdf

------ *Annual Report of the Southeastern Minnesota Farm Management Service*, no. 195. St. Paul, Minnesota: Division of Agricultural Economics, 1951. http://ageconsearch.umn.edu/bitstream/13110/1mr520195.pdf

U.S. Census Bureau. "12th Census of the United States: 1900." Minnesota, Steele County, Aurora Township Enumerations District 123. Accessed March 24, 2014, from interactive.ancestry.com.

"Western Equine Encephalomyelitis." Los Angeles County West Vector & Vector-Borne Disease Control District. Accessed February 10, 2015. http://www.lawestvector.org/wee.htm

Wolesky, Michael. *We Lack for Nothing Now: Czech Settlement in Steele County, Minnesota*. Wolindoo, 2011.

World Reference Atlas. Covent Garden Books, 2004.

Acknowledgements

In the 1980s, Sue Barrett, a friend of Bernadette's, began searching for John and Dorothy's ancestors after John made the remark that he did not have a photo of his grandfather. Sue consulted Internet records and sites like Ancestry.com and even accompanied Dorothy to the Steele County Courthouse to locate birth and death records. Over the years, she sent notes and bits and pieces to Bernadette that later helped to assemble some of this family story. Thank you for getting us started, Sue.

We owe a thank you to Michael Wolesky. His book, *We Lack for Nothing Now – The Czech Settlement of Steele County, Minnesota,* was an eye opener. His research was invaluable as we explored our own Czech roots. It was also helpful as Colleen prepared for her trip to the Czech Republic and the villages of our great-grandparents.

We thank Kim Gengler, Colleen's oldest daughter, who read several versions of the document and challenged us to go deeper into our own stories as well as those of our parents and ancestors.

We thank our editor, Sarah Selz, for pulling the many threads together so that we could tell our story in a more coherent and appealing way.

We appreciate our readers, Sara Thomasy, Darielle Gengler-Hanson and Isaac McGurran-Hanson, for their helpful feedback and enthusiasm for the book project.

We thank Don Gengler, Colleen's husband, for his technical expertise in describing agricultural practices.

The Steele County Historical Society was most helpful in locating information which assisted us in researching our family history.

Finally we acknowledge that we are amateur historians attempting to do the best job we can in recording family history, events and most importantly, our own stories. If there are errors or omissions in the details of dates or historical family events, they are our own.

Made in the USA
Middletown, DE
08 August 2019